MARK BRANDON READ

CHOPPER 3

MARK BRANDON READ

CHOPPER 3

HELL HATH NO FURY LIKE A MATE SHOT IN THE ARSE

𝕁𝔹

JOHN BLAKE

Published by John Blake Publishing Ltd,
3, Bramber Court, 2 Bramber Road,
London W14 9PB, England

www.blake.co.uk

First published in paperback in 2004

ISBN 1 84454 040 5

British Library Cataloguing-in-Publication Data:

A catalogue record for this book is available from the British Library.

Design by www.envydesign.co.uk

Printed in Great Britain by BookMarque

1 3 5 7 9 10 8 6 4 2

Papers used by John Blake Publishing are natural, recyclable products made from wood grown in sustainable forests. The manufacturing processes conform to the environmental regulations of the country of origin.

Every attempt has been made to contact the relevant copyright-holders, but some were unobtainable. We would be grateful if the appropriate people could contact us.

They all hate The Chopper,
They all want to rock and roll,
But their brains are scrambled,
And their courage is on the dole.
They say they're going to shoot me,
But they're talking rather rash,
Because their mouths are passing cheques,
Their hearts could never cash.

HELL KNOWS NO FURY
LIKE A MATE SHOT IN THE ARSE

CONTENTS

THE EDITORS

IN 1991 investigative journalist John Silvester interviewed Mark Brandon Read in Pentridge Prison's top security H Division for a series of newspaper reports. Over almost three years Read has written more than 1,000 letters from both inside and outside jail. These form the basis of Read's best-selling autobiography Chopper, its UK sequel How to Shoot Friends and Influence People and this book.

Silvester has been a crime reporter since 1978. He rowed at Cambridge (in a hired dinghy) and went to Oxford – on a bus.
Andrew Rule is a retired police reporter and failed amateur jockey who currently produces radio 3AW's award-winning breakfast programme.

The editors would like to thank Det. Sen. Sergeant R. O. T. Plumber (retired).

THE OPERA
AIN'T OVER

MARK Brandon Read is one of the most feared under-world executioners and standover men in Australian criminal history. And he is by far the best known, following the runaway success of two volumes of crime memoirs in which he candidly confesses to murder, arson and torture.

This, his third book, was written in a prison cell. At 38, the man known as 'Chopper' faces spending the rest of his life in Tasmania's Risdon prison for a shooting he claims he did not commit.

The response to Read's first two books has been phenomenal. He has become a bizarre celebrity – receiving fan mail from as far afield as England and attracting tourists to the prison asking him to sign copies of his books. A Sydney film company has negotiated rights to the books, and a draft script has been commissioned.

But while Read's fame grows, fed by his remarkable ability to write about the most macabre affairs in a chatty, disarming vernacular, his life continues to be a disaster. The man who has already spent most of his adult years behind bars now faces the probability of never being free again. For Read is one of the few men in Australia's history who has been judged sane but sentenced to jail with no release date.

After being convicted in 1992 of shooting his former friend Sid Collins, Read was 'given the key' – prison parlance for being locked up at the Governor's Pleasure. This sentence is usually reserved for the criminally insane and, in some states, for chronic sex offenders. Read is neither. He admits that he is a dangerous and violent man who has preyed on drug dealers and other career criminals, but he argues vehemently in his defence that he has never set out to hurt an ordinary citizen.

In 1993 Read appealed against his conviction. He was defeated, but has vowed to take the legal battle to the High Court, and is characteristically confident of acquittal.

After being released from Pentridge in November 1991, where he had served a long term for shooting a drug dealer and burning the house of another, he moved to Launceston vowing he would never again be behind bars. It was an empty boast. Six months later he was back in jail, his fantasies of 'peaceful retirement' exploded. His most loyal ally, the woman who had stuck by him for 10 years, was finally forced to agree there was no future in a relationship with a man facing the likelihood of life in prison.

While on the outside, Read rarely worked for a living, finding standover activities more profitable and less taxing. Ironically, it was relatively late in life that he found he did have a talent for making an honest dollar – by writing about his life and crimes and the underworld scene he had known since his days as a teenage tearaway. But the old adage that crime does not pay still applies: any author's royalties Read has earned have been spent on lawyers fighting to clear him of the Collins shooting.

Meanwhile, as Read continues to protest his innocence on the Collins matter, detectives from Melbourne and Sydney have said they want to interview him over certain unsolved major crimes on the mainland.

For this book Read has obtained confidential and exten-sive prison files relating to him under the Freedom of Information Act. These include psychological assessments, prison classification and discipline records. They provide a fascinating insight into the way a maverick criminal has dealt with prison bureaucracy for almost two decades – with a pungent mixture of childlike innocence and street cunning, hoodlum bravado and quaint, old fashioned politeness. Will the real Chopper please stand up?

Read is the son of a strict Seventh Day Adventist woman who instructed him in fundamental Christianity and a war veteran father who instructed him in firearms and fighting from an early age. He was disciplined severely at home and bullied and ridiculed at school because he was a slow learner and because of his mother's unusual religious convictions. The young Read responded first by impressing his peers with his tolerance of pain then, as he grew stronger, with his willingness to inflict it on others.

He concedes that he was not always the most skilled streetfighter, but he built a fearsome reputation for his willingness to inflict violence with absolutely no regard for the consequences, physical or legal. But there is a price for that brand of insanity: Read carries terrible scars from being repeatedly shot, stabbed and bashed – and has spent most of his adult life in jail. And for what? For all his bizarre cult status, his 'kill-and-tell' revelations have distanced him even further from both mainstream society and the underworld. Even if he was willing, neither world would now accept him.

Read, with characteristic audacity, declares that none of this worries him. 'While you keep getting up, you aren't beaten,' he says. 'The opera ain't over 'till someone shoots the fat lady.'

John Silvester and Andrew Rule

CHAPTER 1

THE STORY OF TANYA AND EDDY

'SHE PUT THE PLAN TOGETHER
AND SET HIM UP NICELY,
COLD-BLOODED AS YOU PLEASE'

OF all the evil women I've seen, and I've seen some bad ones, the worst was not only one of the youngest but the best-looking.

Her name was Tanya. She had an angel's face, but underneath the good looks she was a cunning, treacherous slut. I have never worked out how some women can have so much going for them and yet turn out such twisted bitches. If Tanya had played life straight, good men would have done anything for her, but that wouldn't have been enough. She didn't just want more. She wanted it all.

Tanya started out as a teenage runaway. Then she was a street pro, but instead of ending up in the gutter with a needle in her arm she climbed the ladder to massage parlours, then escort work and working as a stripper. She was a busy little bitch at the best of times. A real lady of the night, who loved her 'work'.

She had a schoolgirl face and a tomboy haircut but she was, I admit, very cute and spunky-looking. Then she met Eddy and retired from the game, because she didn't have to earn an 'honest' dollar any more.

Tanya had been selling her body since she was 12 years old, and she fell in love with Eddy when she was 19. Seven years in that game would harden anybody, but I think she was tough as nails from the beginning, then got even tougher.

Eddy was an up-and-coming gangster from the western suburbs of Melbourne. He drove a Porsche, wore expensive jewellery, carried a gun and was a pretty tough Italian crook. He made his money from drugs, and was making plenty of it. He was popular and respected, even feared, and his reputation was growing as fast as his bank balance.

But Eddy had a problem: his looks. He was wealthy, well-dressed and a pretty flash bloke who was just a bit too good-looking for his own good. The girls loved him, and this burned Tanya up.

Tanya was a jealous lady. In fact, she had the heart of a scorpion and the brain of a snake, a tiny package of pure evil and vice, and it all came spitting out when she found out Eddy wanted to move her out, so that he could move a 17-year-old in.

Eddy's lust would sign his own death warrant.

IT was Tanya who approached me about Eddy. She put the plan together and set him up nicely, cold-blooded as you please. She told me what she wanted and she gave me the key to his flat.

When I walked in the door with Dave the Jew, no one heard a thing. When the bedroom door opened, Eddy looked up to see me and a sawn-off, double-barrel shotgun. He had his head between Tanya's legs, and as he looked up at me, Tanya screamed, 'Kill the dog, kill the dog!' He thought she was screaming for him to kill me, but he was wrong ... she was screaming for me to kill Eddy. But he must have realised the truth when she lifted her leg up and kicked out with her foot, catching him hard across the face.

I gave Eddy a slam across the face with the barrel of the shotgun. Dave stepped in and gave him a slight touch-up, then handcuffed him, hands behind his back and face down.

Tanya was on her feet by this time. She took me straight to the stash, and what a stash it was. There was cash, jewellery and drugs. She wanted the drugs, which was fair enough. Let her kill herself. There was a pound of pure speed and a 28-gram bag of heroin. She took that plus some personal jewellery and all Eddy's gold chains – there were about 10 – and added them to the dozen she was already wearing.

There was about $4,000 in notes. That went in my pocket. Tanya told me Eddy had two guns and another $4,000 hidden in the car. She wanted the Porsche, but she got the keys and gave them to Dave and he went and got a .45 calibre automatic and a Colt .32 calibre revolver, plus some ammo and a bankroll of cash that would choke a horse.

While this was going on, Tanya was busy. Wearing only high heels and a dressing gown, she was running around packing her clothes – and grabbing anything else she wanted. Dave helped her pack the Porsche up with her things, and the various goodies she had her eye on. Then I said to her, 'Hang on, we will take Eddy with us, so you can clean the flat out in your own sweet time. He won't be back.'

We had planned to take Eddy back to a friend's hotel in Fitzroy where we could deal with him in the cellar in our own way. It was a proven winner for us. But Tanya wanted to be there for the kill. Her, eyes were ablaze. 'Let me watch,' she begged. Then she started to stab the sharp heel of her stiletto shoe down into Eddy's back and shoulders, and she got down and bit him so hard it drew blood.

She wanted to stab him. We had to pull her up. Then she said, 'Sit him up and you can screw me while he watches. Come on, Chopper.'

It was all getting a bit kinky for me. It was quite clear that Tanya was a sadistic whore and the whole thing was getting quite sleazy. I am a head hunter, not a perverted killer who has sex with the wives and the girlfriends of men just before they are about to die. Dave wasn't pleased. He looked at me in a way which indicated total disgust.

Tanya said, 'Let me come. I know where he has three buckets of junkie gold hidden.' By this she meant stolen rings and jewellery, sold to Eddy by junkies in exchange for drugs. She also said there was another $5,000 and three more guns hidden with the jewels. Little Tanya said Eddy rented a house in Footscray where he kept his gear. 'I only know the street, not the number,' she said.

I told her: 'Tanya, you can't watch nothing.' She went mad and kicked the shit out of Eddy's face. 'Let me bite the dog's dick off,' she screamed.

'Look,' I told her. 'We will take him. You stay here and pack your new car and we will ring you later.' She wasn't happy, but she had no choice.

Dave and I took Eddy, who seemed resigned and quiet, almost accepting death. Maybe the fact he knew he had been set up by his own girlfriend had numbed him. Whatever the reason, he was very peaceful. He even told us the number of the house in Footscray. So, instead of taking him to a pub in Fitzroy, we took him to his own rented house. We had him wrapped in a blanket. We got him into the house and found all the goodies and more.

We also found an electric nail gun.

Dave was convinced he was holding out, but I knew he was a broken man. Tanya had broken him. Nevertheless, I put a nail into his kneecap. But before I could reach the other knee, Dave said: 'Hold on.'

Eddy's eyes were closed. He was dead.

People don't die from a knee capping. But Eddy was a heavy user of speed, and the combined effect of the drug, the emotional and mental shock, and the nail in his knee just blew his heart apart.

The nail gun was a nuke, but we kept it. And that's not all. The house had about $20,000 in handyman's tools stored in one bedroom.

We had to stack 'Dead Eddy' away in the freezer of a friend's pub. From the time we grabbed Eddy until the time of his death was about

36 hours. I'm cutting this short. I think it is wise for all concerned.

We got rid of the body in a rather unique way. Eddy was left in a strange place or, should I say, four strange places. The Jew handled that. Meanwhile, I had to handle Tanya, which was fortunate for her.

You see, what dear little Tanya didn't know is that the Jew said she had to die. But I've never killed a female, and I never could. Don't ask me why, but to me it just didn't seem right. I'm a bit of a fuddy duddy in that area.

So I didn't kill Tanya, but I did go to see her and got her all sorted out. She had sold the contents of Eddy's flat, and taken what she wanted. She told her friends and the busy-bodies that Eddy had run away with his 17-year-old slut.

I said to her: 'If you don't get in your new car and get your nice new things to some safe place, you are going on the missing list. I don't want to hurt you, but my blue-eyed mate thinks you'd go well in a hole.'

Tanya was not stupid. She said she was always planning to go interstate, so she may as well get moving right away. As we parted company she said: 'Chopper, don't you want to screw me?' I looked at her and said, 'Tanya, you're one chick I don't want to screw or screw with. See you later.'

I mightn't have screwed Tanya, but she screwed me. I later heard that Eddy had kept $30,000 cash stuffed in a vacuum cleaner – a hiding place that Tanya had suggested but conveniently forgot while I was around. So I guess she had the last laugh on all concerned.

Tanya went west eventually and had a business involvement in the escort agency area. She has a string of strippers for bucks' night, hotels and clubs, and is doing very well financially, I hear.

Although his death and the way he finished was rather sad, shed no tears for Fast Eddy. He was a heavy drug dealer, a killer who specialised in overdosing junkies who upset him, talked too much, or owed him money.

Yes, Eddy was bad news. But he had nothing on his darling Tanya. She was, to my way of thinking, one of the most dangerous and evil women I have ever known. I have seen plenty of sick-minded, black-hearted, coldblooded sluts, but Tanya was the Devil's personal whore. That chick was the Princess of Pain.

FOOTNOTE: While Eddy was lying in the freezer for five days waiting for disposal, me and the Jew did another two other jobs of work.
   Busy, busy, busy. Ha, ha, ha.

CHAPTER 2

IT'S A DOG-EAT-DOG WORLD

'WHEN WE HEARD OF THE FIGHT, WE WENT TO THE HOME OF TAFFY AND SPOKE SEVERELY TO HIS FATHER, BROTHER AND UNCLE, PUTTING ALL THREE IN HOSPITAL'

IT was 16 November 1972, the day before my 18th birthday. I felt a sense of great expectation. It had the promise of being a grand day indeed.

We met at the Try Boys' Youth Club in Surrey Road, Prahran. Terry the Tank arrived late, as always, and I gave him a dirty look as I sat in the old barber's chair in our headquarters underneath the stage. There was a large cubby room under the stage which dated back to when the building had been a theatre, before being turned into an indoor basketball court for the youth club.

The room was less than seven feet high, but about 20 feet long and 10 wide. It was nearly dark, with only one small light globe. There was a window but we kept it covered. It was our own little patch.

It was here that we held court and completed our pre-battle meetings. Me sitting in the barber's chair, Cowboy Johnny Harris to my left, sitting on a stool, and Dave the Jew pacing the length of the room, eager for combat and complaining that these pre-battle meetings were just a waste of time. Terry the Tank would just sit there, a little worried about what the hell I was up to.

Dave the Jew had a World War I, British-made Scott and Webley handgun, which was a lovely bit of work. I had a sawn-off, double-barrelled shotgun. The Cowboy had two steel bars about 12 inches long and Terry the Tank had a claw hammer. I also had a World War I British Army bayonet. We weren't boy scouts, but we always liked to be prepared.

The four of us were waiting for Solly the Jew and a bloke nicknamed Reggie the Rat, for on this particular day we needed extra combat troops.

Solly and Reggie arrived. Solly had a beautifully made petrol bomb, and the Rat had a lovely set of meat cleavers. It had all the signs of a wonderful day out.

We were all set for a bit of action because the Cowboy had bashed the uncle and father of a tough gang leader from St Kilda named Taffy, and the St Kilda boys had vowed to take revenge. They had even come over to Prahran and started a fight in the bar of the South Yarra Arms Hotel, looking for him. We were all in the bar of the Bush Inn Hotel at the time, and when we heard of the fight, we went to the home of Taffy and spoke severely to his father, brother and uncle, putting all three in hospital. The Jew wanted to shoot Taffy's mother, but I put a halt to that. It wasn't good manners to shoot mothers, even in St Kilda.

Messengers went back and forth and the result was that the Surrey Road Gang had been challenged to blood combat. We were to meet behind the St Kilda Football Oval. But I changed the plans, saying that as they had challenged us, we would fight on our home turf, on the railway tracks running between the Hawksburn and South Yarra railway stations.

It was going to be a bloodbath. Needless to say, I looked forward to it, and expected everybody in the gang to do likewise.

We had promised that it would be a fist fight and there would be no weapons. What a joke. I had always held the view that anyone who didn't bring a gun to a fist fight was a poof, or at least a fool.

Taffy had a friend from Preston, a famous streetfighter named Sugar Davis. He is now dead, but in 1972, the name Sugar Davis was known and feared. He was a streetfighting legend.

Taffy had also promised to bring some of the other toughest streetfighters in town to back him. Most of them didn't turn up because, even as a 17-year-old, I'm proud to say that in the gangs of Melbourne I had a reputation as a cheat who couldn't be trusted in a fight, and they all feared a foul ambush. They somehow suspected that I had no intention of fighting on the railway tracks and would have had some dirty tricks planned.

Well, what happened that night even I couldn't have planned. The six of us walked out of the Try Boys' Youth Club and headed up Surrey Road. We were under the railway bridge, just past the council depot and garbage incinerator, when three cars headed towards us and screamed to a halt.

It was Taffy, his dad, uncle and brother, Sugar Davis, a bloke called Snakes, and two other blokes I didn't know, nor liked the look of.

Solly the Jew turned and ran, Terry the Tank froze in his tracks, and Reggie the Rat took one look and headed off after Solly. Which left just me, Dave and the Cowboy to face the onslaught.

Taffy had a baseball bat, and all the others appeared to holding lengths of iron pipes.

Sugar Davis stepped up and said, 'Right, which one is Chopper'. When I said it was me, he said, 'Well, let's see how good you are.'

'Pig's arse,' I said. 'Dave, shoot the bastard.' Bang, bang, bang. The Jew let three bullets go, all missed Sugar Davis, but one of them hit Taffy.

Terry the Tank unfroze and ran in screaming, swinging his claw hammer fast and hard. Snakes and Taffy's brother fell to the ground, pissing blood. Taffy's dad and uncle were next. Terry was going crazy, Cowboy was bashing Taffy while he lay on the road with a bullet in his arm. He was beating him with two steel bars. Cowboy might not have been a heavy thinker, but he was a heavy streetfighter.

I pulled out the sawn-off shotgun and aimed it at the head of Sugar Davis. He said, 'Go on, shoot me, you weak rat.' Sugar was a tough bastard. The Jew yelled out, 'I will', and put a bullet in his leg. I then stepped in and bashed Davis around the head and face with the shotgun.

The two other tough guys who came with Taffy's crew just stood there and watched it all like stale bottles of piss.

The four of us then ran off up the road, having won the day in grand fashion.

No one gave anyone up so the law didn't get involved. Ah, the fun-filled days of youth. It was a great day indeed ... apart from a small matter of cowardice under fire. Our next job was to decide on punishment for Solly the Jew and Reggie the Rat.

In gang wars, like any war, you have to have discipline from the troops. Two of our people had cut and run before the battle had even started. In a war they would have been executed, but we were only kids and wouldn't go that far. And, after all, they were friends, and I have always been known for my compassion.

We let Solly off with a fine – and a sound flogging. We broke nearly every rib in his body with a cricket bat. The fine was $1,000. He came from a wealthy family so he could afford it. As it turned out, Solly was never a great one for physical violence. He was a rather meek fellow, but he still ended up making his mark in the underworld. A scorch mark, to be precise.

Although Solly later became quite successful in the rag trade, he always had a healthy 'sidelight' to his main business. He was the master of the Jewish Bonfire. In other words, he was an expert torch, who helped people to collect on their fire insurance. As Dave said, Solly was the best at organising the Jewish Fire Sale. He became the Chopper Read of arson.

Dave and I once watched a fire in a factory in South Yarra and Dave laughed and said, 'Good golly, it's Solly.' Sure enough, there was little Solly asking the firemen questions as they were trying to put out the fire in his grandfather's factory. God bless him.

Anyway, back to the story. Reggie the Rat still needed to be punished. He had a pet fox terrier, so we caught it, killed it, cut it up and cooked it on Reggie's barbecue in his own backyard, with Reggie standing there in tears.

Then came the master stroke. We made Reggie eat his own fox terrier. But it wasn't all bad. We had garlic salt, cooking oil, salt and pepper, plus American mustard. After all, we weren't savages.

The rest of us had two dozen cans for the feed. Dave thought it was the height of high comedy. Poor Reggie was bawling like a baby as we forced him to eat his own pet.

I told him, 'You acted like a weak dog, so maybe eating your own dog might give you a little courage.' You are what you eat, they say.

I did not partake in the feed, but the Cowboy did, and he pronounced the foxy quite tasty. The Cowboy would have eaten dirt if you let him.

Two weeks after the puppy picnic, Reggie and two of the Richmond boys attacked me as I drank in the Morning Star Hotel. Dave the Jew and Cowboy Johnny Harris were across the road getting takeaway food while I was being kicked to bits in the pub. They returned to find me looking like a busted open watermelon. On my recovery, we went to Reggie's home while he was out and killed all his pigeons, about 60 of them. One way and another, poor Reggie didn't seem to have much luck with pets.

The next night Reggie the Rat and the same two Richmond nitwits, Johnny the Wog and a giant Greek we didn't know, attacked me again in the bar of the Bush Inn Hotel. But this time I was waiting. The three of them were beaten into the street by the

Cowboy, Terry the Tank and the Jew. I took my physical exercise that night by breaking ribs with an iron bar.

Reggie the Rat died in a car accident in 1974, and the Surrey Road Gang went to the funeral and wake. They were great days. I miss them.

Incidentally, Old Taffy had a long memory. In late 1974, he was still keen to even the score. He and his gang attacked me in the car park of the Croydon Hotel, which is a long way from St Kilda. I was being kicked near to death, but I had managed to drop one of my attackers with a broken beer bottle to the face, when Bobby Lochrie, one of the best streetfighters in Melbourne and a top bloke, backed up by his crew, came to my rescue. The fight then got under way on a much more even keel.

I've told the story before about how police from all over were called to break it up and they, too, got involved. It was a great battle, with all of us fighting together. Me and Loxy escaped back into the bar, where we drank and watched the whole car park get arrested and tossed into the back of assorted divvy vans. A big police sergeant walked up behind us as we watched all the fuss through the bar room window and said, 'You two bastards were involved in that.'

We turned to look at him, with our faces covered in blood, and Loxy said, 'No, Sarge, we were in another fight in the lounge.'

The sergeant said, 'Well, no more fighting.' The truth was that the police didn't have enough cop cars and divvy vans to arrest us all.

In fact, there had been a fight in the lounge. Four of our mates had nearly wrecked the joint. We went back into the lounge where Loxy started another punch-up. He was always a sucker for a good time. When the police came again, the fight was over, the lounge bar was a mess of broken and bleeding men, and there was broken glass and windows everywhere. The same big sergeant came up to me and Loxy and said, 'You two were involved in this one.'

Loxy just said, 'No, we were in the blue in the car park.'

Well, the cops had had enough for one night. They closed the lounge bar and kicked us out of the pub. But we weren't arrested.

Police in those days had a far more balanced attitude to youthful frolics in pubs and car parks. They knew not to take these matters too seriously.

After all, a good time was had by all.

THE BALLAD OF REGGIE THE RAT

Reggie the Rat ran away,
But we knew we'd catch him another day,
Solly the Jew did the same,
So we taught him it was no game.
When we got Reggie, he wasn't alone,
He had his fox terrier guarding his home,
The Cowboy gave the dog a kicking,
Then the Jew told the Rat to give it a licking,
I fired up the barbie, but the food tasted poxy,
'Cos we made the Rat eat his own foxy.

CHAPTER 3

THE LAST GOODBYE

'MY CARDS WERE MARKED LONG BEFORE
I MET MARGARET AND, IN THE END, IT WAS
TOO MUCH FOR HER TO BEAR'

SADLY, I have to say that the woman I love and I have split up. Margaret stuck with me for more than 10 years, and in that time I was on the outside for all of 13 months.

It seems that all I was able to give her was torment, pain and tears.

I loved her, yet all I managed to do was hurt her. I would have rather died than put her through the agony that she had to endure. It was just part of my life. It seems that if you get close to me, you get hurt. I can't explain it.

My cards were marked long before I met Margaret and in the end, it was too much for her to bear.

I am sad, and I will always love her, but my life is a sinking ship, and I cannot ask someone I love to drown with me. To do so would be to turn on the very love that brought us together. I don't want to lose her, yet I know I must.

To hold on in the face of the nightmare of a life is self-centred and cruel.

Margaret has stuck with me when I have done stupid things. She has stuck when people wanted to kill me. She stuck when I was inside. There is no one as loyal as little Margaret. If most of the two-bit crims had her dash, guts and courage, they would never tell tales out of school in police stations. She has more guts than most gunmen, more loyalty than a blood relative.

Margaret has been a part of me for so long that it is like losing part of myself. But to try to hold on to the love under the circumstances would be to poison it in the end.

Even if I win my legal battles, there is no promise that things will ever change for me. This is not the life for a woman like Margaret. She has so much to offer and is so full of life that she shouldn't waste it on a legal loser like me.

She bullied and nagged me and gave me hell, all because she could see the truth about other people and how they were using me. She was so frustrated that I couldn't see that some of my so-called friends were out to take advantage. If I had only listened to her then perhaps I wouldn't be sitting in Risdon Prison now. I've had a lot of time to think about that lately.

We had a new start when I left Victoria. We had some money and the chance to settle down. We could have lived the quiet and contented life in Launceston. But I ended up with some people who tried to manipulate me and live off me. It was Margaret who saw through them but I was too much of a fool to listen. She put her whole life into trying to make my life better, but it never worked.

In return, I only hurt the one I love.

I now know that if there was a next time it would probably only be more of the same, so it is time to end it, no matter how much it hurts. Margaret has gone back to Melbourne and taken our dog, Mr Nibbles.

I've lost my girl and my dog. Now if that ain't pain then I don't know what is. She told me once that I was the man of her dreams, but all I ever gave her was a nightmare.

Sorry, darling. I will always love you, but it was doomed from the start.

SHE'S GONE AWAY

She's gone away and left me,
Yes, she's calling it a day.
We both know it's for the best,
But I really wish she'd stay.
She was the one who held my hand,
When there was no one there at all,
She watched me climb the mountain,
And then she watched me fall.
Take care, darling, in whatever you decide to do,
And remember there's someone here,
Who'll never stop loving you.
I wish I could return and go right back to the start,
Baby, it's hard to explain the tears from a broken heart.

CHAPTER 4

A PRISON GUIDE TO BREAKFAST ETIQUETTE

'I AM WELL VERSED IN THE TRAINING OF
SMALL DOGS ON THE OUTSIDE AND
VIETNAMESE AND OTHERS IN THE JUG'

ON Sunday, 13 December 1992, in the remand yard of Risdon jail, I am delighted to have the pleasure of viewing a spectacle of high comedy. It is the sort of thing which can only happen in jail, and a Tassie jail at that.

There are three Vietnamese in the remand yard. They are pretty rare down here, a little like Tasmanian Aborigines.

Any rate, for the sake of the story, I will call them Huey, Dewey and Louie. They are rice eaters from Western Australia, very quiet, peaceful and polite and no bother at all.

But, in jail, little annoying habits can really grind away, and the rice eaters had one habit which really got up a few noses. Every morning at breakfast they go through each slice of toast, feeling each slice with their fingers, picking out the choicest bits for themselves, leaving the much-mauled remains for the rest of the crew.

This happens for every prisoner, except for me, as I am well versed in the training of small dogs on the outside and Vietnamese and others in the jug. But a crew of three local boys in remand trying to spread their Vegemite over the top of Asian fingerprints is all too much, and to cut a long story short, there are some heated words over the cold toast.

The three Vietnamese chaps revert to their old stock standard: 'Me no understand what you say, me no speak English.' A punch is tossed and one of the Aussie boys cops a smack in the mouth.

Bread and butter knives are produced along with verbal abuse and threats flying on both sides of the breakfast table. It certainly wasn't like this in the Brady Bunch. Breakfast ends without any further harsh words or actions, but there is bad blood and, patron of the pugilistic arts as I am, I am keenly looking forward to round two.

The three local boys are set on teaching our friends Huey, Dewey and Louie a lesson in manners, Aussie style. Naturally, they plan a sound flogging for them. But they have never tangled with Vietnamese before. And they don't know that your typical rice eater has no formal grounding in the gentle art of self-defence under Marquis of Queensberry rules.

Huey is a tallish, slightly solid fellow, Dewey is an average size, slender chap, and Louie is a Vietnamese version of a Leprechaun, about four foot nothing and about five stone wringing wet.

The three local champions are average size for Aussies, so they have height and strength on their side. These local lads spend the morning trying to gather assorted weapons for the upcoming battle: rubbish bin lids, broom handles and so on. The Viets watch every move they make.

I try to explain, as gently as I can, to the local boys that a sneak attack is the only way to go, but when the shit is about to hit the fan, it is still a case of them turning into schoolboys. The lads stand there yelling things like, 'Well, go on, do you want to have a go?' I'm thinking one of them might add any moment, 'You and me, behind the shelter shed after school, one on one.'

Obviously Huey, Dewey and Louie have done their education elsewhere, because they jump straight in and grab the assorted weapons the Aussies have spent all morning acquiring. The fighting is fast and furious, with flying kicks and Bruce Lee impersonations, and broom handles and rubbish bin lids flying everywhere.

The screaming Vietnamese fight tooth and nail as a team and the local lads are very much taken by surprise at the courage and violence of their opponents.

One local boy ends up on the ground with Dewey, who sinks his teeth into the Aussie's neck and nose. A flying rubbish bin lid cuts the hand of another local lad. There are punches and kicks all round. The Aussie boys give a good account of themselves, but they are trying to fight fair in the face of total insanity.

Little Louie gets a boot in the mouth and all six cop each other a sound touch-up. But in the end the team work, dirty tricks and violence of the Viets beats the strength and guts of the Aussies. It is the first Aussie-Viet battle in Risdon's history, and it teaches the locals a valuable, if painful lesson. The next time around, it will have to be blood and guts all the way. I am much impressed with the efforts of the Viets. Two of the locals have to go to hospital to get patched and stitched up. All six end up around the corner in N Division, the Punishment Division, with the promise of revenge and the next round to follow.

I'm tipping that next time around the Aussies will win, for they now know it is all the way or not at all when fighting our Asian friends.

But the Vietnamese will keep coming back, and if they get hold of the right killing weapons, there will be bodies dropping.

Anyway, their little altercation was the high point in my time in the remand yard. I thought it was high comedy. A little bit of slapstick humour. Or should that be chopstick humour? Ha, ha.

CHAPTER 5

LIFE IN THE PINK PALACE

'IN TASSIE THERE ARE THREE CLASSES OF
CRIMINALS: WHITE COLLAR, BLUE COLLAR
AND NO COLLAR'

TASSIE'S Risdon Prison isn't such a bad place, really, in spite of my unkind remarks about it. Alcatraz it ain't, but there are some pretty solid boys doing time here at the old Pink Palace, as we call it. Shane Hutton, Neville Taylor, Rocky Devine, to name but a few. The Vietnamese Mafia, Huey, Dewey and Louie, have now been convicted and have to do six months for robbing some Chinese people. Whether it is on the mainland or in Tassie, it appears that the Chinese and the Viets just can't get along. I taught Huey, Dewey and Louie to sing 'Australia is a wonderful country', and 'We love Bruce Ruxton'. Ha, ha.

The screws aren't a bad lot. There is a relaxed and easy-going attitude that I like. The big boss of the jail, the captain of the good ship Risdon, is Governor George Lawler, a big old boy who looks like he has been fighting all his life. A tough old bugger, but a fair man, he is always telling me to plead guilty. I said to him once, 'Would you plead guilty if you were in my place?'

'Certainly not!' was his reply.

Jail governors, no matter what state you are in, are all cut from the same barbed wire fence. You can jump all over them, but they cut the shit out of you if you get caught.

One ray of sunshine here is the female psychologist down at the hospital. Her name is Jo Hunter, and she looks like she belongs in the pages of *Penthouse* magazine. She is in the right line of work, because watching her walk around the jail is causing mass nervous breakdowns.

In any jail in Australia, you will always find a few characters, and the Pink Palace is no different. There is one bloke here who I will call 'Double Bunger' Freddie. His name is Freddie Plumstead and he had a girlfriend with a healthy appetite in matters which normally happen in the bedroom.

Now old Freddie was nothing if not generous, and when the girlfriend mentioned that she was interested in taking on two men at once, Freddie contacted an escort service and got the services of a local stud for $280. Now the escort was supposed to keep the girlfriend busy at one end while Freddie attacked from behind. But the escort, Jamie, was sadly unable to rise to the occasion and, to top it off, Freddie heard his girlfriend say to the wilting young man, 'Give me a ring when Fred's not about.'

Well, Fred spat the dummy, and anything else that was in his mouth at the time, and gunplay followed. Fred held the young man at gunpoint and got his $280 back, and he let a few shots rip as well.

Personally, I thought gunplay was over the top. He should have just taken him to the small claims tribunal instead. As for the girl, she sounds like the life of the party.

There are plenty more characters here. The trouble with the jail is that it is built like a toy prison. The Pentridge car park is probably bigger than the whole of Risdon. The boys playing cricket here have to be careful that they don't hit the ball too hard, in case they hit some passerby walking his dog near the jail.

I am going to fight hard to win all my legal battles but, if it goes against me, I could be in worse places than Risdon.

IN Tassie there are three classes of criminals: white collar, blue collar and no collar. There is no doubt that down here the prince of the white collar crims is the disgraced accountant, Colin Room.

Many professionals who hit a legal hurdle drop their bundles and do their time hard. But not Colin – he even refused parole because he was too busy on the inside with his various jobs. He was writing a history book on Tasmania and involved in the prison debating team.

But in December 1992, time ran out for Colin. He had served his sentence and he left, swearing on his stockbroker's wooden leg that he was out of funds and had not been able to squirrel anything away in his days as a bent money man.

I will miss Colin's cheerful face around the place, as he was a very pleasant chap. He was the master of the flying conversation. You'd see him walking towards you and, with a wave and a smile, he would start chatting away with the latest news, information and gossip. The only thing you didn't get in these snippets was an up-to-date weather forecast and the latest betting on the day's TAB meeting.

These conversations would begin at about 20 to 25 paces apart and continue until he was about 25 paces past you. He was a fast talker and could jam quite a deal in those 50 steps. Those flying chats always amused me as he never seemed to be able to talk while he was standing still. He liked to talk to people as he rushed around Risdon like an amphetamines freak on roller skates.

He was like a politician – always talking, walking and carrying an armful of papers. In fact, I personally think that Colin should be in Parliament and many politicians should be in Risdon.

In many jails it is said that one or more tough inmates actually run the jail. In Risdon, Colin ran the place, not because he was tough, but because he was an organisational dynamo. Most screws are lazy by nature and Colin took over many major duties that a prisoner should not have been asked, or even allowed, to do.

I quite like this strange little man, with the smile of a Mexican politician and the glib tongue of a used car salesman. During the jail football season, they would video tape the game and Colin would do the commentary. It would then be replayed to the whole jail that night.

It was a major comedy, to hear this upmarket, private school, cultured voice calling a game where players were kicking and punching each other half to death. He may not have been king of the jail, but Colin was the king of comedy.

I wish him well in his future ventures. He is not a bad bloke. Criminally speaking, he is not someone I would put in the boot of a car. You wouldn't get money out of him with a crowbar.

ON my daily walks to the prison hospital from the remand yard to get my vitamin tablet I found, much to my delight, seven big, fat snails, bloody big buggers. Anyone who has been to jail knows that all prisoners become first class scroungers and learn that anything they can find to use they will grab with both hands.

Now, the sight of seven snails was too great a temptation to me. I scooped the blighters up and asked one of the screws to boil up some water for me. I placed the snails in the water and let them soak for about 10 minutes. I then got some more boiling water and gave them another 10 minutes. That seemed to slow them down, in a manner of speaking. They were easy then to pop out of their shells.

I got hold of some silver paper, some salt, pepper, garlic powder and a spoonful of butter. I didn't have a French cookbook so I had to do the best I could. In prison, Nouvelle Cuisine is anything cooked by a first-year apprentice cook. I got the recently deceased snails, minus their shells, and wrapped them in the silver paper, with the salt, pepper, butter and garlic powder. I placed the lot on the grill under the big toaster in the remand yard dining room. I gave it about 10 minutes, five on each side, then I pulled the parcel out and took them back into the remand yard.

All in all, I must say that they didn't taste too bad, perhaps a touch oily and chewy. I was particularly proud of the garlic, which gave them that French flavour.

They went down well, so every day I went to the hospital I would keep my eyes out for a few snails. In the end I found the spot. They seemed to have a little patch near the hospital garden where they would gather. I was able to scoop them up, making sure not to grab too many of the little green pellets around them.

I felt I was getting the hang of the French cooking. In fact, with my experience with meat cleavers I thought that when I got out of jail I could go into the culinary business.

I was confident, perhaps too confident, about my cooking skills. The little buggers finally had their revenge. I had plenty of time to think about my mistakes as I was sitting on the toilet. I know about severe stomach pains, having been stabbed in the guts once or twice, and let me tell you, the snails were tougher than a sneak knife attack.

I was shivering and shaking and thought I was at death's door. I have suffered bad cases of Bombay Bottom, at the hands of Mad Dog's curried vegies in Pentridge and Slim Minogue's chilli powder delights, but that pales into nothing compared with the revenge of the killer snails.

It was then I learned a very important lesson about cooking the more exotic dishes. If one insists on eating garlic snails, one should always know that the snails themselves have not gobbled a gutful of snail bait. The little green pellets turned out to be snail poison and the buggers I had been eating were the gung-ho survivors of more chemicals than Chernobyl.

IN my experience, the best sort of screws in any prison are the ex-army, navy and airforce blokes. They have been there and done that, and seen it all, and they don't seem to have anything to prove. It is the same with ex-boxers. They are normally good blokes who don't get into punch-ons to prove their worth because they have already done that in the ring.

Vietnam vets seem OK, although some can be a little crazy. But in the prison service it seems that the bigger fool you are the higher you go up the tree. There are contradictions to every rule, but generally, what I say is true. The prison service is hardly a vocation. Ask a group of schoolchildren what they want to be when they grow up and not one will say, 'I want to be a screw and look after tattooed psychopaths in a cold and damp prison.' Face facts, it is not like being a brain surgeon or a jet pilot, is it?

Generally speaking I get on well with prison officers, because I am polite and can tell a joke. Screws get bored, like everyone else, and they like a bit of a laugh, but sometimes it is a little like trying to converse with the mentally retarded. Now, don't get me wrong, I will never be remembered as a genius, but fair dinkum, compared with some of these prison officers, I could have been a Rhodes Scholar. They would have struggled to be road workers.

Crims and screws agree on one thing: that the people who run prisons wouldn't know if a tram was up them unless you rang the bell.

THERE is a delightful senior Prison Officer here called Dave Oakley. He is a nice bloke, and like many of us he has a paranoid fear and distaste for creepy crawlies such as spiders and snakes and the like. A great deal of tasteless practical jokes have been played on Mr Oakley, involving assorted creepy crawlies, dead and alive. This has filled him with horror, outrage and a fair degree of panic. One day a fellow prison officer found a freshly dead tiger snake and, in the name of good humour, curled it up near the front door of Dave's car in the prison officers' car park. Dave was knocking off work and left the prison, only to return minutes later, ashen-faced, and without a word to his colleagues, he went to the prison armoury and grabbed a shotgun. He then walked back out of the jail towards the car park, took aim and blew the snake to Kingdom Come. His fellow officers, shocked, but still smiling, said, 'Dave, it was already dead.'

Mr Oakley, the colour returning to his face, turned and said, 'Well, it's a damn sight deader now.' He then picked up his bag and went home. The practical jokes in relation to Mr Oakley and creepy crawlies stopped around the same time that the tiger snake met its second death.

Dave later said that as far as he was concerned there are no such things as empty guns or dead snakes and, personally, I tend to agree. I wouldn't care if it was a dead snake or a rubber one, I'd shoot it just to be on the safe side.

I was called in recently by one of the top men in the jail and he said that after reading my mail it would appear that I was trying to write some sort of book without permission from the appropriate authorities. I reeled in horror. Perish the thought, an inmate of Her Majesty's Prison, Risdon, trying to write a book. Outrageous! In reality, I think that they all knew another book was in the wind and they were only flying the flag.

I wonder if they'll want autographed copies when it comes out?

IT WAS 13 May. Fistic combat was in the air. The combatants were Craig 'Al Plonko' Ferris, a Sydney crook, doing time for rape, and Kevin 'The Drunk' Clarke, doing not a real lot for God knows what. Ferris was in the remand yard on appeal and Clarke was there for reasons that even puzzled him. Al Plonko was a fitness freak, with the fighting ability of a wet soapy sock. Clarkey the drunk had been a handy man with his fists until the grog and ill-health had kidnapped him and took him to the land of the semi-dead. But the old drunk had guts, and was eager to rock and roll, in spite of the fact that Al Plonko was twice his size and in better physical shape.

Let me tell you, this was not a fight that would take top billing in a Don King Production at Caesar's Palace. It wouldn't even get a gig on a Bernard King Caesar salad, but on a boring day in Risdon, it pulled a crowd.

Both men took off their shirts and, bare-chested, proceeded to shape up, if that was the word. It reminded me of a schoolboy sparring match between two 10-year-olds. It was a most civilised affair, nifty little jabs and hooks that swept through the air with little danger of hitting a target.

Al Plonko decided to liven the affair by throwing a few kicks out which would have made Sir Robert Helpmann proud. The sparring contest proceeded to get mildly violent as some glancing blows hit the mark on both sides. The close quarters work began, with a few semi-hard punches starting to hit their marks on both men's heads and faces. Then there was the break as more circling and long range jabs became the order of the moment. I was about to take a nap when suddenly a glancing right hand from Al Plonko caught the drunk on the right side of the jaw. Kevin staggered and started to step backwards, then, with eyes rolling, he fell backwards to the cement, and hit the deck heavily, with the back of his skull smashing in the cement like a sledge hammer. He lifted his head and tried to get up, but his eyes rolled again and his right arm and legs started to shake, rattle and roll. He was having some sort of epileptic fit, accompanied by choking sounds and violent shaking.

It was not a good look. The comedy of the fight had taken a sad and distressing turn.

Al Plonko, feeling he had won some major and worthy victory, began to get a little bit lippy. Meanwhile, prison officers came from everywhere to see what had happened. There was so many of them there at one point it looked like a union meeting. Eventually Clarkey was bundled on to a stretcher and taken to hospital. Big Frank Jones, a jolly joker by nature, was not happy and ordered that Al Plonko be taken around the corner to the punishment division, N Division.

As quick as it had started, the drama was over. After a comfortable night in the Royal Hobart Hospital, Kevin 'The Drunk' was also sent to N Division to recover.

This is May in Tassie and the winter comes early. In N Division there is no central heating. The moral of the story is don't get sat on your arse and have a fit at Risdon.

What a fiasco.

WHILE inside I have got mail by the truck load. Much of it is nice but some is rather puzzling. I have heard from literary critics and lounge chair intellectuals telling me that my books have no real message. Well, first of all, the only literary critic I really care about is the cash register, and when it stops ringing I will know I have hit a false note.

As far as intellectuals are concerned, an intellectual is someone who spends all his time giving other people the answers to questions he didn't understand in the first place. They go through life dreaming up new ways to fix problems that they themselves created.

I never went out to write a book that had a special message. If you played it backwards on your record player it wouldn't tell you what really happened to Elvis, although I believe that my life, when viewed from a safe distance, does have several messages, such as don't cut your ears off and never be friendly with Sid Collins.

But, regardless of that, people write to me complaining that after several readings of my first two books, they felt they had to contact me to raise several points regarding my attitude to this or that. For goodness sake, I am in the bin doing a monster stretch for something I didn't do and these people want some academic discussion. They must be kidding.

The truth is that all I ever wanted to do was write a cook book. I was going to call it: 'How to Kill Them in the Kitchen'.

A PSYCHOLOGICAL point that I am forced to ponder is really more of a question for which I know I will never find the answer. Why is it that when I am in jail and locked up like a rat in a trap, and totally unable to take advantage of any romantic situation offered to me, I manage to pull more pussy than a Chinese restaurant? Yet, when I am free and at large, girls of loose morals bite holes in screen doors trying to get away from me.

I mean, all the good luck I have with girls seems to find me when I am in jail. I get it all when I am behind bars rather than when I have one, if you get the drift. If there is a God, then he has a twisted sense of humour. That's why there are women banging on the gates trying to get in to visit me, others ringing the prison crying over the phone pleading to talk to me, and others writing me pornographic love letters. But when I am on the outside, things change. If I was standing in a room full of nympho-maniacs, I could swing a cat and not hit a soul.

They seem to be waiting in the wings for the news that I am in jail – and then they attack me with outrageous offers of pleasure and pain that would make the silver gun rapist blush. Mad Micky said to me that I'll die a lonely man with a thousand chicks I've never met, crying at my funeral.

Of the several hundred love letters I have got in jail, I have developed a good filing system. You may remember that while in jail I have to go without a private secretary. The letters from old, ugly or fat chicks go in the bin. Cruel, you may think. Well, put it this way, if you are silly enough to write a love letter with a photo included to a self-confessed arsehole, then you better make sure you are good looking, or it's straight into the old round filing cabinet.

I have replied to some letters, and write to a small fistful of outrageously good-looking young ladies. Just because I've got no ears doesn't mean I've got no taste

John Le Carré once wrote that some people simply elbow their way into a novel and sit there till the writer finds them a place. There is one young lady who did this to me. She didn't set out to elbow her way into my book, but she ended up elbowing her way into my life. She has been writing to me for a year. She sends me short stories: strange, weird, freaky fairytales that sweep the reader off in an X-rated version of Disneyland. She has a fertile imagination and a scallywag sense of humour. Next to Dorothy L. Sayers, this little honey has become my favourite female writer.

Lady bar-room story tellers are rare and her stories always have a slightly naughty twist to them which appeals to a man behind bars. Her name is Tauree and she is a bloody good chick, so while I may slag off most of them, girls like Tauree are the exception.

Another good and loyal friend is Mary-Ann from the Tax Department. I told her if I get out I wouldn't mind taxing the pants off her. I think I won her with the line, 'Have you ever stuck your tongue in an ear that wasn't there?' Goodness, I am a suave devil.

It's quite amazing. Here I sit with a no-eared toothless head that even a mother wouldn't love and I've got the screws of Risdon shooing the sheilas away with a stick. God's idea of a practical joke? I can't figure it out.

ONE day back in May I was called up to the Governor's office. I certainly don't like these visits as they are rarely purely social. When I am walking to the office I always wonder what I have done wrong. It is silly really. Here I am worrying like a schoolboy on his way to the headmaster's office, when there is precious little they can do to me. The courts have already done their worst – throwing away the key, so to speak, by giving me the Governor's Pleasure sentence, which means my release date is the 12th of never, if my appeal fails. (Editors' note: Read's appeal did subsequently fail.)

Anyway, Chief Prison Officer Frank Jones and Senior Prison Officer K.D. Salter, the boss of the Prison Officers' Cricket Club, were also in attendance, with Deputy Governor Graham Harris at the helm.

I stepped into the room and gave Governor Harris a snappy salute, as inmates at the Pink Palace are required to do. I waited in trepidation for the bollocking I thought I'd get for some perceived misdeed. But what followed left me quite shaken.

The conversation was most friendly and civil. I would even describe it as warm, with the Deputy Governor even breaking out in a smile. I kid you not, the man actually smiled. I saw his teeth and everything. I nearly fell over. There was even a hint of laughter. While there was no suggestion that the tea and scones were on their way, it certainly turned out a pleasant chat.

I found it hard to believe there was no catch, as it is my painful experience that jail governors are at their worst when they are smiling. I have noted on my psychological travels that some of the strangest beasts in the world are prison governors. They are a race on their own.

I walked out of the headmaster's office most confused. I had misjudged the nature and temperament of the dear Deputy Governor. Had my previous evaluation of the man's character been flawed? Could Graham Harris be hiding a sense of humour that had escaped me on previous meetings? Jail governors are a never-ending psychological puzzle that I am yet to understand after about 18 years of careful observation.

The screws in any jail are always a strange mix of the plain weird, the soldier of fortune type, bible bashers, drunks and the classic Aussie bar-room story tellers.

One in Risdon who is a classic story teller and yarn spinner is Dave Oakley, the man who doesn't like snakes. He is a tough old boy who does his job well but, because he has a good sense of humour, he gets on well with the inmates. He has a heart of gold and a dry wit which can double me up in fits of laughter.

There are other prison officers here who like to think they are heavy thinkers. One of them loves to sit down with me and have huge psychological debates about the pros and cons of the inner workings of the human mind. He has locked me into some debates which have left me in dire need of a Panadol and a good lie down.

He likes to climb inside your head and pick, pick, pick at your brain. My method is more likely to creep up behind you and go whack, whack, whack with an ice-pick.

Having lurched out of huge, deep and exhausting mental debates I sometimes run into a Mormon prison officer who wants a big rave about God. Sometimes I don't know whether this is a jail or a big pink debating society. All in all the prison officers in Risdon are not a bad lot. Screws and coppers seem to be cut from the same cloth, mentally and emotionally. Most have got a good sense of humour. It can be a valuable weapon. A screw without a sense of humour won't last long.

Now, I love a visit and the other day two detectives from Melbourne popped in for a chat. It was a pity they had come over to investigate a bit of trivia. The poor chaps had been assigned to check out some flapdoodle about a prisoner who committed suicide in Pentridge some years ago.

Sean Downie was the bloke who hanged himself and the investigation at least gave the two Melbourne detectives the excuse to get away from the dusty corridors of St Kilda Road and get over Bass Strait on a day trip.

It was all due to the anti-nuclear fruitcake, John Dixon-Jenkins, and the teacup revolutionary, Jeff Lapidos, from the Prisoners' Ratbag Reform Action Faction. These two men seem convinced that Downie was murdered. No, young Sean had the bad manners to decide to take early parole while in the cell next to mine, and I have been left to live with the wild rumours that I helped him on his way, or that I am covering up for corrupt prison officers who may have been involved in his death.

The reason for the conspiracy theory related to my bored and wicked mind, and Dixon-Jenkins's paranoia. After we bade a fond farewell to Downie, John got his cell – the death cell, as he called it. John has always been a paranoid believer in conspiracy theories and would not sit still for the suicide theory. He demanded that I tell him the 'truth' on the matter, so naturally I decided to give him both barrels.

I told John that the taxi driver Sean Downie had murdered was a high-ranking member of the Masonic Lodge and that Downie was strung up and set on fire by a Masonic death squad operating in the ranks of the prison staff at Pentridge.

John Dixon-Jenkins, a bright and sincere man, not known for his sense of humour, reeled back in horror. You see, I have a tattoo on my right forearm that reads 'Brethren Black Chapter, Antient charge v1.4' and another tattoo on my left forearm that reads 'Sublime sons of Hiram Abriff'. Perhaps that's why John always felt that I had some sort of affiliation with the Masonic Lodge.

Of course, my whole story was pure rollicking rubbish, but John was horrified, and for a time believed he was on some sort of Masonic hit list. To tell the truth, in all the excitement, I forgot to tell John that I was pulling his leg, and the poor mad bugger has been screaming blue murder ever since. All I can say to John is that it is all rubbish. But even so, he'd better mind how he goes or the Freemasons will get him.

The truth was that Downie was a young crook who came into Pentridge charged with the murder of a cab driver. They put him in the top security space station, Jika Jika, in 1987.

He didn't like the place and freaked right out. He wasn't the only one. Only months later five prisoners, including my former best mate, Jimmy Loughnan, started a fire which killed them all and led to the closing of the electronic zoo. So you can see that, in 1987, Jika Jika was not the place to be if you were a little unsettled in the brain box department. They put Sean in Unit Two next to me and he flipped right out and took his own life. Big deal. That was not unusual in jail at the time, but the funny thing was that Downie was not going to leave anything to chance.

He set fire to his cell, the mattress, sheets, blankets and newspapers, then hanged himself. I suppose he did it in that order – it would have been a little difficult the other way around.

Just as well he didn't take rat poison and shoot himself as well, or those with suspicious minds would get really excited. I might add that the smoke from the fire almost killed us. The inconsiderate blighter didn't even think of the hole in the ozone layer when he decided to jump off the perch.

Of course, some people considered it odd that some prison staff had visited Downie shortly before he decided on the Viking funeral. I was called to the inquest but I couldn't shed any light on the matter. How could I? I couldn't see anything for the bloody smoke. Any rate, I was asleep during the whole sordid event. Years of experience have taught me that it is best to sleep when people are hanging themselves. Some inmates always believed it was murder. Downie was a psycho so it could have been anything. It is none of my business, but the nickname for suicide in jail is early parole, and for what it's worth I believe that Downie simply took early parole.

Even though I told the coroner I knew nothing about the Downie affair, there were some unkind people who suggested that I magically appeared in Sean's cell, and gave him the big helping hand.

Need I tell the fair-minded reader that this is, as you would imagine, foul gossip and slander of the highest order. There have been suggestions that there was some bad blood between Downie and me. Nonsense. We were not blood brothers and we had no plans to share a cottage by the sea together after our release, but we were not enemies.

It seems if I have the misfortune to have my cell next to a depressed pyromaniac with a neck rash, people think I have killed him. The gossips will wag their unkind tongues.

All I can say is to my knowledge there was no foul play involved. When it comes to death, whether it be murder or suicide, the three wise monkeys had the right idea: see nothing, hear nothing and, most importantly, say nothing. As I said, I was asleep at the time.

THE LONELY ROAD

The bubbles of fortune, bursting in the air,
My life's a walking time bomb, but I don't really care,
I tried to do it nice, but I only broke her heart,
Ain't no way to go back, or mend what's torn apart,
So I'll just keep on going, and try to do it right,
But with both eyes open, it's still hard to see the light,
I am the man I am, and I guess I'll never change,
No matter what I do, or how I rearrange,
But why do I keep on laughing, in the face of all my hell,
Even the Devil wouldn't go to where I'm forced to dwell,
So I walk a lonely road, with a heart that won't forget,
And still it's true to say, I ain't got no regrets.

CHAPTER 6

LADIES AND NOT-SO-GENTLEMEN

'I HAD THE FEELING THAT IF I'D FLUKED
WINNING A GAME, I WOULD HAVE HAD TO
SHOOT MY WAY OUT OF TOWN'

I MET Billie in a country pub in Tasmania, on the coast. She was a big chick, well built and with a top suntan. In Tassie, they don't worry about skin cancer – they think UV rays is a new Space Invader game.

When I walked into the pub, Billie was wearing a pair of ladies running shorts which must have belonged to her baby sister – and they must have shrunk in the wash – a pair of thongs, a tee shirt and a very bold smile.

This was not in the formal dining room, you must understand.

Billie was full of laughs and jokes and then she challenged me to a game of pool. She said, 'Do you want a bet?' I said okay and she nominated $50 a game. I put my $50 down and said, 'Where's your cash?' She said she didn't have the money but suggested that if she won, she would get the cash, and if I won, I got to get inside her running shorts, if you get my drift.

This was the strangest bet I had been involved in, if you leave out playing Russian Roulette with Vietnamese in Footscray. I asked her if she was serious, and she dropped her pants and poked her bottom in my direction and said, 'Check that out.'

I did, and decided immediately to accept the wager.

We began to play. Never in my life had I wanted to win a game of pub pool as much as that afternoon. We played and we drank all afternoon. She beat me six out of six games. It cost me $300 and a headache. I vowed never to play her again. She was good looking and cheeky, but too good for me. I gave up and went to the bar. I said to the laughing locals, 'Why don't you play her?' They told me they all had and that no one had beaten her since she was 12.

The only way she could get a game these days was to offer the sexy side wager, and as far as anyone knew, she had never needed to pay up. She only played passing strangers because the locals knew they didn't have a hope against her. She could make between $200 and $500 a week, depending on how many mugs she could stooge.

The less she wore, the longer mugs like me would stand there, losing game after game, hoping to get her pants down. She told me that winter is the worst: 'When you're all rugged up, the boys lose interest'.

Billie was built like an Amazon princess and she was only 16 years old. What really made me worry was that I found out her dad owned the pub and was standing behind the bar.

I had the feeling that if I'd fluked winning a game, I would have had to shoot my way out of town.

'Tough Tony'

Tony Franzone was shot six times, twice in the back of the head, in a professional hit outside his home in the Melbourne suburb of Mt Waverley in May, 1992. Franzone was with his de facto wife and was about to take his 11-week-old son from the back of his car when he was ambushed. He was a heavy gambler who enjoyed the company of gangsters.

'TOUGH TONY' Franzone wasn't tough at all. In fact, he was as weak as piss, and everybody who knew him knew it – hence the nickname. But Tony did play a small role in organised illegal gambling in both Carlton and Fitzroy. I guess he could be called part of the Carlton Crew, the gang of would-be Mafia types who made their money out of illegal gambling and drugs. Tony liked to give people the impression he was connected with the right people. He thought he was a real mob guy, just like in the movies.

I was introduced to him in Carlton and he squeezed a $100 note into my hand as if he was tipping a waiter. He was a two-bob millionaire and a real would-be gangster. He was basically harmless, and seen as a likeable joke. When people would say: 'Here comes Tough Tony', the trouble was that poor old Tony didn't see that it was a joke. He started to believe he was a tough guy. He owed money and believed that his reputation and name would cover his bad debts. But he just didn't have a reputation, except in his own imagination.

The poor stupid bastard thought that real life was like the movies and he was the star who never got shot. I used to have chicks drop his name to me, as a means of impressing me that they knew some heavy people. I mean, this poor slob had a lot of people convinced he was some sort of Mafia tough guy. He told a couple of people in a nightclub one night that Chopper was a 'stone killer' and that 'we are gunna have to whack that guy'.

His mouth and his imagination were his worst two enemies. He ran a few illegal card games and a few clubs, or so he claimed. He struck me as a bloke who couldn't run a stocking. He gambled and got into big debt with some of the main figures in the Italian gambling world. For them, violence is a way of life, not something from the movies.

He thought he could bullshit his way out of anything. He was a dead man, even when I met him years ago. He had big debts and there were people who were looking to collect. He was living on his wits and his mouth even then. He was a loser and it was always just a matter of time.

I used to bump into him at the Chevron nightclub. He always had a few chicks with him, paid by the hour to impress his mates. In the company of the big boys he was just a hanger on.

Whenever he saw me he would try to give the impression that he was a great personal friend. He'd shout me drinks and sling me money, and introduce me to whichever girl or girls he had with him on the night. If I wanted to blow my nose on his shirt he would have paid for the privilege. The guy was a suckhole.

Poor old 'Tough Tony'. Sooner or later, when you play gangster, you'll be called upon to back it up. He got blown away in May, 1992, to make an example for other people who didn't pay their debts. And because he was a pest, simple as that.

Neddy spills his guts

Arthur Stanley Smith was one of Sydney's most feared gangsters. He was involved in murders, heroin distribution, prostitution and police corruption. He was given the green light by corrupt police to commit armed robberies and virtually any crimes he wanted in the 1970s and 1980s. He is now serving life for murder and has become an Independent Commission Against Corruption protected witness. Smith's autobiography, 'Neddy, The Life and Times of Arthur Stanley Smith', was published in mid-1993.

I WAS amused to see that Neddy Smith, one of Sydney's better known criminal identities, was going to give evidence to the NSW Independent Commission Against Corruption about his involvement with a host of Sydney police. He has told the ICAC about his various Alice in Wonderland adventures with the NSW boys in blue.

I don't know why Sydney crooks don't stick to what they know best, pimping for whores and selling drugs to kids. Every time you see a Sydney crook on television, he is either lying in the street after being killed by an imported Melbourne hitman, or giving Crown evidence against some poor bastard.

The biggest and most feared underworld killer Sydney ever saw was

Chris Flannery, and he was from Melbourne, and an idiot at that. Neddy, bless his heart, is also trying to jump on that boring old bandwagon, claiming to know who killed Flannery and why.

Flannery was put off by a Melbourne hitman. I know the bloke who did it, how he got rid of the mortal remains and the reason for the killing.

I can tell you the Melbourne gentleman I am referring to roars with laughter every time he hears one of these razzle dazzle Sydney boys taking the bows or dropping hints over Flannery.

Neddy should kick a few goals by talking to the ICAC. Hush hush secret talks behind closed doors – they'll all love it. Sometimes it is a case of the paranoid talking to the mentally ill. Neddy has been good for a giggle for many years and he is not letting us down now. Sydney crooks watch too much television.

Being frank about Huttons

ANOTHER mate of mine here at Risdon is Shane Hutton. His younger brother Andy used to knock about with me and the boys on the outside, and sometimes go shooting with us, as I've mentioned elsewhere.

Andy was a sight – drunk, with a loaded semi-automatic high-powered rifle – a sight I wish I had never seen. Andy had a plate in his head, metal that is, not the dinner variety. He would blast away with scant regard for life and limb, sending the rest of us diving to the dirt to avoid the worst massacre ever seen in Tassie. How he didn't kill all of us, and why I didn't put a big dent in his plate, I will never know.

Anyway, Andy's big brother Shane has become a good mate on the inside. He is a top bloke with a friendly smile and a warm personality. He is a solid bloke, a hard man with a good heart. He is doing life for double murder. He isn't a bad man, just a good bloke who had a bad day.

Shane has shown me great kindness since I was dumped in here. He is a good style of chap all round and one to have on your side if things turn nasty. He is a gentleman from the old school who understands that it is poor form to give someone up in the police station. These days when you meet a solid bloke, you should write down his name, as they are a dying race of men. In fact, the good blokes' club is the smallest club in the world.

Rocky Devine

ONE of the most colourful characters here at the Pink Palace is Robert 'Rocky' Devine. Tassie is split into two halves, the north and the south, and they are like separate camps. While Mad Micky Marlow is the most colorful character and best known alleged crook in the north of the state, Rocky is the best known in the south. God knows what would happen if they got together.

Rocky thinks it is the height of bad manners to give anyone up at any time. I found him to be a good style of bloke. He is a top footballer and coaches the jail team. The games are replayed over the jail video. While my little mate Neville Taylor is the goal kicking star, Rocky leads the charge. The games are a mixture of high comedy, Aussie Rules and punch ups, which makes the replays absolute must viewing.

While Mad Mick has falsely been accused of being a safe cracker, a slanderous statement if I have ever heard one, Rocky is thought to be a bank robber. Another tall story, no doubt. Rocky is a big, mean-looking bugger, with as many tattoos as me but less hair. And he has ears, which puts him in front of me in that regard, a point he was quick to point out when I mentioned his thinning hair line.

The solid men of Risdon have as much dash and guts as trims that I have met anywhere, but the dogs in the place are as low as anything I have ever seen. When I first came to the Pink Palace, I thought the place was a joke, but it has grown on me. I would just prefer that I wasn't here, that's all. But as old Ned once said: 'Such is life'. Ned Kelly, that is, not Smith.

Raymond John Denning

Raymond John Denning was one of the most notorious criminals in Australia, a NSW prison escapee who became a folk hero for his attempts to expose flaws in the prison system. Songs were written about him before he was arrested by police in 1933. He turned police informer and died after he was thrown out of the witness protection scheme in 1993. Mystery still surrounds his death. Some people say he was killed; others say it was natural causes. Read couldn't care less.

I WAS much pleased to hear of the death of Ray Denning. The witness protection program and 30 pieces of silver didn't do him much good in the end.

'Denning was a good bloke' . . . 'Ray Denning is as solid as a rock. He is one bloke you can trust'. . . if I heard that once, I heard it a thousand times, and every clown thought it was true. Denning spent his whole adult life riding high in the criminal world and the NSW prison system. He rode a wave of overwhelming popularity. He was a legend, his name was part of criminal folklore. My mate Mad Dog put his neck on the chopping block for Denning because a thousand old-time solid crooks from one end of the nation to the other swore that Ray was a good bloke.

The Sydney underworld held Denning up as their prime example of a real hard man. A staunch, solid crook who wouldn't give an inch and who would never talk in a police station. He was loved and respected. Crims are like any other group around the place - they love to look up to someone, to have idols. And to many crims, particularly in Sydney, Denning was an idol.

But in the end, when Denning faced real pressure, he folded. He rolled over and did whatever the police and the Crown Law Department wanted done. After a lifetime of standing in the sunshine with a thousand men patting him on the back, he found himself standing alone in the cold, with no place to run and no place to hide. Like so many others, he simply crumbled, shrivelled up to the nothing he really was all the time. These fairweather gangsters turn dog as soon as the sun goes in behind a cloud. As that old bloke in Dad's Army used to say: 'They don't like it up 'em'. Ha ha. The more popular a man is, the less I trust him. The more friends a man has, the more questions I ask about him. I am still trying to find out if Sydney has ever produced a famous crim, with the exception of Mad Dog.

Ray Denning should be a lesson to us all. The next time we hear someone say: 'Yeah, he's a good bloke, you can trust him', just remember Denning. As far as Sydney is concerned, Ray Denning was about the best their excuse for an underworld could produce. You'd get more support from an underwire bra than the underworld up there.

I'd rather be backed up by one hated arsehole who can stick fat than a hundred popular showponies who can't keep their mouths shut. I can name a lot of crooks, including myself, who could turn around tomorrow and say I know where the body is buried or I know who did it, just to get out of jail. Traitors are shot in wartime, but in peacetime they are encouraged and protected.

The great Australian moral code is a thing of the past.

Mental as anything . . . the nurses, that is

WHEN I was first put into the mental hospital in Melbourne by my mother, it was a horrifying experience. I was in a lock-up security ward and life was not nice. Plenty of pills and needles to try and keep you under control. The male nurses looked more like nightclub bouncers than sisters of charity.

In the 1970s, the mental hospitals around Australia made our jails look tame; violence was part of the treatment. There were 20-stone male nurses dressed in white except for their black boots. They handled the mentally ill with great care and compassion, and a boot in the head, followed by a needle in the arse. If you so much as farted out of place, you would be whacked out with medication.

I have never really experienced the sort of ill-treatment in prison that's even worth mentioning in the same breath as the mental hospitals I have been in.

Even though they wanted to keep me sedated I did have some run-ins with some of the staff during my stay there. One night, a group of the hoons decided to get into me and give me the big needle. Now I had already had all my medication and, not without good reason, I protested at these apes trying to use me as a pin cushion.

I was about to be given a giant touch up by this lot when a big, mean-looking patient, with the strength of 10 men, rushed in and came to the rescue. He made short work of the night shift staff and saved my neck. He ended up getting my needle for his efforts and some electric shock therapy the next day. There is quite a tale to be told about this fellow, but I have promised him I will be discreet.

What they did to him for putting his head in and backing me up just wasn't nice, and I won't forget him for the efforts and what he copped on my behalf. His name was Geoff and I still owe him.

Geoff is now a top knockabout. He went on to be a nightclub bouncer and then went to London and managed a rock band.

After that he went over to Ireland to manage a team of strippers. That turned into total chaos, with Geoff being arrested. He came back to Australia and played in various rock bands, putting his guitar over the heads of a few before he would play the gig. He is still involved in the scene, managing a few strippers. I have been to a few strip nights organised by Geoff, and let me tell you, they were all wild nights.

Geoff is not a crook, but he's met them all. After he helped me out in the mental hospital, I was moved out of the lock-up ward and taken to an area where men and women patients were able to mix freely. I was 15 years old and quite advanced physically. I was well-educated in matters of violence, but still shy in matters of romance and sex. In fact, I never played funny buggers with a chick until I was 18 years old. So what I saw in the mixed ward was a shock to me. They all slept in separate areas, but they mixed freely in the day rooms and gardens, and wandered in and out of each other's sleeping areas. The place was like a rabbit warren with all the maddies humping each other, raping each other and attacking each other. I am glad that my old dad rescued me from that place.

The worst thing I saw there was to watch a big male nurse tease a patient for no reason. The nurse would take the bloke's hat, a Collingwood Football Club beanie. The poor chap was going insane. He kept crying, begging and pleading with the nurse for his beanie, but the staff member just kept laughing and saying: 'Sorry, but it's against the rules. Only North Melbourne beanies are allowed here'.

The nurse was having what he thought was a joke and the other patients were laughing. I was full of nut house drugs and couldn't even get out of my chair, but I could see what was happening quite clearly.

The patient who was being teased began to bang his head hard against the wall. Once, twice, three times – until he split his skull open, and still the nurse would not return the beanie. The poor patient kept banging his head until there was blood everywhere. Then three male nurses came out and he got the big needle to calm him down.

They would give you this needle which would leave you a helpless and dribbling mess, shitting and pissing your pants, unable to move.

It was hell. Some of the staff would take sexual advantage of some of the female patients. Thank God all that rubbish has changed in our mental hospitals now. I am told things are much better now, and just as well, because it couldn't be worse than it was.

Funeral for a friend

THERE was one sad point when I got out of Melbourne's Pentridge jail, way back on November 14, 1991. I was given parole just three days before my birthday and I had told a mate, Andrew Shadwick, that if I got out we would have a reunion drink on November 17, my birthday.

But 'Shaddy' died on that very day. I was shattered. I hadn't seen him since 1987 when he, Mad Micky and me went to Bojangles Nightclub and nearly got in a gun battle with a group of would-be Mafia hoons.

Both Micky and Shaddy stayed staunch even when guns were drawn and I knew they were both real mates with a ton of guts.

Andrew was a fun-loving giant who could fight like a thrashing machine and a bloke who stayed solid as a rock in a police station, unlike so many other tough guys I could name. He had a heart of gold and fists of iron. You can't replace a bloke like Shaddy. I had already arrived in Tassie and we were supposed to meet in Launceston.

Even though I was right there I didn't go to the funeral. A wake was held at the Outlaws Motorcycle Gang club house and, while I went to that, I didn't go to the real funeral. I have been funny about funerals ever since me and Dave the Jew had that small ceremony at the Prahran Swimming Pool where we deposited the ashes of our great friend, Cowboy Johnny Harris.

While I have no problems in killing a guy, going to a friend's funeral gives me the spooks. I think they are bad magic and something I would avoid at all cost. I know there were many who thought I was unfeeling not to go to Andy's funeral, but I know Shaddy would understand. However, I will attend the funeral of an enemy at the drop of a coffin lid. In fact, I would buy a ticket from a scalper to attend Sid Collins' service, or even to wave goodbye to his missing kidney.

I've noticed with funerals that half the bastards who show up weren't even close friends of the poor bugger in the box. Anyway, to me the last farewell is a private matter. I do not go to say goodbye to a friend in the company of a hundred strangers. It is how you treat a person in life that counts, not how many tears you shed after he is dead.

My mate, or should I say former mate, Amos 'The Witch-Doctor' Atkinson, wouldn't even mention the name of a dead friend. He thought it was bad magic. It is the same with me.

Ambrose Palmer and me

I'VE mentioned before that when I was 15 or 16 years old I used to train at the gym of world champion boxing trainer Ambrose Palmer in West Melbourne. He was a wonderful old bloke and a good mate of my Uncle Eddy. He also got on well with my Dad, so I was looking forward to having Ambrose help me with my fistic style.

The gym had a great atmosphere. Boxers, sportsmen, crooks, scallywags, coppers, local politicians and TV personalities all called in at times. They all loved to watch the training and sparring and have a chat to Ambrose. It really was a big open house. Ambrose was not only the king of boxing trainers, but a living legend. He always had time for people, and was a soft touch for a sob story. He was always ready with a helping hand for anyone going through rough times.

Ambrose looked at me in the ring and said I fought like a kamikaze pilot, and I still don't know if it was a compliment or an insult. All I ever did was charge in and throw punches at a hundred miles an hour, regardless of the damage that was inflicted on my young self.

Ambrose told me I would either kill someone or get myself killed in the ring. He told me it was a waste of time trying to teach me boxing, as I was a suicide merchant who wouldn't listen to any advice. I had sparred over 20 times with men, all older and bigger than me, and I was proud to say I always managed to spill some of their blood in these battles. But Ambrose didn't like my style, and after a sawn-off shotgun was found in my carry bag by some sticky beak, he asked me to leave. It wasn't even my gun; I was just minding it for another bloke.

But in spite of the fact that my dreams of being the world's first earless boxing champion were cruelly dashed, Ambrose and I always remained on friendly terms.

I saw him in Footscray in 1977 and we had a cup of tea together. He was a grand old man and a great Australian. He was also just a bloody good bloke, an honest knockabout who could deal with anyone from pickpockets to prime ministers. He cared about people and helped drag many out of the gutter. Many people who would have ended up as losers were helped by Ambrose and went on to live good, normal lives. If there really is a heaven, I am sure Ambrose is there now.

A protected species

In 1987, the biggest and most powerful heroin dealer in Melbourne was a man I will call the White Ghost. He was from a wealthy Jewish family and lived in a luxury penthouse apartment in St Kilda. He drove an assortment of luxury cars and made no effort to conceal his wealth. He was always seen in the company of glamour ladies and had his money invested in illegal gambling houses in Carlton, massage parlours, restaurants, nightclubs, cafes and factories in the western suburbs. He also had a slice of a jewellery business.

The Ghost was a multi-millionaire, and thought to be untouchable. He was the subject of a federal-state police investigation that lasted years but didn't produce any results. Many police and criminals believed he would never be caught.

One reason for his charmed life was that he was also a top police informer acting for some detectives in the Victoria Police. So while some police wanted him behind bars, others wanted him free to let him give up other crooks. It was very odd, but not an unusual set of circumstances. Police often let some good crooks run if they give them good mail.

I ran into a classic example of this in the Chevron nightclub in St Kilda. Mad Charlie had known the White Ghost for many years and they were not friends. The two of them met up that night and a wild argument started. They were screaming at each other at the top of their voices in another language.

I was never a great debater and I never liked the White Ghost at any rate. Besides, I was acting as a bodyguard for Mad Charlie, so I pulled out a five shot .32 calibre revolver and aimed it at the other bastard's thick head.

I was about to pull the trigger when a plain clothes copper stepped in front of me and flashed his badge. It was the most amazing thing. He just said: 'Put it away, Chopper'.

The police weren't with the Ghost. They were watching him, but his watchers had become his bodyguards. Any move against him was a move against their investigation so, like it or not, they turned into his unpaid bodyguards.

I was not arrested. I was simply asked not to shoot the prick, and being the well-mannered chap I am, I put the gun away. But it made me wonder about things. In order to investigate him and try to arrest him, they save his life - and thank God they did, as they saved me from a life sentence. They weren't going to let me shoot him, but neither were they going to arrest me for attempting to shoot him.

The White Ghost has been a powerful underworld identity as well as a police informer. But his money and his connections won't keep him alive for ever. One day he will run out of people to sell down the drain ... and when that day comes, he will be found in one.

No buts about Bobby

ROBERT Lochrie has been a tried and true friend since our teenage years together. A former pro boxer and nightclub bouncer, he's a bloke who gets into a bit of trouble now and again, rather than what I'd call a criminal. He was as loyal a friend and ally as I have ever had, and as a back up in any type of fight, he was the best. I could ask for no-one as solid as Loxy in matters of violence.

He backed me up over the years and his violence was matched by his closed mouth if matters ended up in a police station. He saved my neck numerous times by flying into fights when I was outnumbered.

It is a pity that most of the best stories about Loxy must remain untold as it would place him in legal hot water. All I can say is that not all the blokes that Loxy and I had to deal with made it to the hospital. Bobby always liked to finish a fight with one for the road - a running jump, with both feet ending up on the head or neck of the fallen enemy. From experience, let me tell you that it is a bloody dangerous weapon used in hotel carparks.

I've seen this guy cut his way through a crowded bar with a broken beer bottle to get to my side when the odds were against me, thus saving my neck.

Loxy is a happy-go-lucky, fun-loving guy who happens to be a bit of a nutter. He would follow The Chopper to the grave, and on several occasions, almost did. To him it was all fun.

I once saw him head-butt a local smartarse by smashing through the side window of the other bloke's car. Picture it, an EH Holden, all doors locked and the windows wound up tight, with some ratbag at the wheel making rude gestures towards my good self and Loxy. Robert went over and was most frustrated to find the doors locked, with this ratbag indicating to me and Loxy, with hand and mouth gestures, some sort of unspeakable sexual act.

What he got for his trouble was Loxy's head crashing through the window and into his own. He was then pulled out through the window and kicked in the head and neck until he lay there like a used dish rag.

Me and Loxy went into the pub where we remained for two or three hours and the smart arse was still lying by his car. We didn't know whether to call an ambulance or Windscreens O'Brien.

CHAPTER 7

PUPPY LOVE

'HE WAS DESPERATE TO MEET HER AND
OFFERED ME A GREYHOUND FOR HER
ADDRESS'

CHAPTER

PUPPY LOVE

ONE of the more interesting visitors I've had in Risdon was the girl who liked my first book so much she had the image of the cover tattooed on her shoulder.

Her name is Karen and she is a little honey with an obvious artistic touch. She arrived wearing or, should I say, almost wearing, a very tight little dress. I must say she is a little glamour pussy.

She told me she has only read two books in her life, *Chopper One* and *Chopper Two*. Well, surely that is enough higher learning for anyone. After reading my literary efforts, her cultural cup runneth over.

Karen showed me her tattoo while standing on the seat provided for visitors. I must say I wasn't expecting a strip show, but it was done in the nicest possible taste.

Little Karen, also known as 'The White Dove', hitchhikes down to Risdon from Launceston to see me on a regular basis. I can tell you I am most concerned for her wellbeing, as she does not rug up warmly for the trip. Whenever I see her she seems to be wearing less and less.

Now, one day she was standing on the Midlands Highway with her thumb and her chest out and two cars stopped and the two drivers wanted to punch on to see who could give her the lift. Karen wisely ran off and was rescued by a lady driver who turned out to be a very religious woman who insisted on giving Karen a stern lecture about wearing suggestive clothing and accepting rides from strange men.

Karen didn't have the heart to tell the woman that she was on her way to an all-male jail, and not a prayer meeting. The woman insisted that the two of them share a little prayer in the car to save the White Dove's soul.

They say travel broadens the mind. I like Karen. She hitchhikes down here rain, hail or shine wearing just enough to avoid arrest. She makes me laugh with her wonderful stories about what she gets up to. She was once called for jury duty, and didn't want to fulfil her community service, so she went to court half drunk and wearing a pair of short shorts and a tee shirt which read: 'I'm a virgin, this is a very old tee shirt.' The funny thing was that it was a rape case – and she got picked. Once on the jury, of course, Karen took her duty seriously. Launceston is a very small town. She knew the so-called victim and was very unimpressed with the Crown case.

The White Dove is very public spirited like that, always trying to help out. In fact, after showing me her tattoo she made me an offer which was hard to refuse – although I'm not sure when I can take her up on it. She wants to be my driver when I get out of jail.

Considering that my last driver, Trent Anthony, got $500 a week and I paid for all food and drinks, who wouldn't want the job? Karen promised me if she got the job, she wouldn't verbal me in a police station, wouldn't give Crown evidence against me ... and she was at pains to point out that there may be other fringe benefits for me in the deal that Trent Anthony would never have dreamed of, or at least I hope he didn't.

As she wiggled away from the visiting area, I thought about how all the good offers happen to me when I am on the inside. I thought about the offer. I can hardly say: 'Karen, you're hired.'

Karen is a looker and has heaps of dash, but at the moment she has a small problem – she hasn't got a licence. She may be able to drive most males into a frenzy, but she can't drive anything with an engine. She is already taking driving lessons, and has told me she has already had to sit one stiff oral exam which she passed with flying colours. On the strength of that, I am most keen for her to audition for the job.

At the moment she can't back out of the driveway without hitting the letterbox, but she is so enthusiastic I am sure she will get there in the end.

The trouble is that she was getting lessons from some lovesick teenager, who insisted on trying to run his hand up her leg while she was concentrating on driving. He did it once too often while she was going around a corner at a fair rate of knots. She spun the car, hit the gutter and broke the axle. Serves the young pimply git right for being too horny for his own good.

Karen is a good sort who loves the greyhounds, going shooting and having a drink. She can outdrink most men I know. But she has done a few things which make me wonder if all is well in the brain box department.

She had two dogs, her own pets, and her landlord told her to get rid of them. But instead of taking them to the pound she shot them both in the head, and dumped them in the blackberry bushes.

One of the dogs wasn't dead, and came back with the slug in its head. It was moaning and she didn't have the heart to shoot it again, so she put sleeping pills in its food. That didn't work, so she finally did shoot it again. But it still wouldn't lie down, so she let it have it with the axe and then buried the body.

Somehow, I don't think I want to get on the wrong side of this one.

She writes to me every day. When she was a kid, she used to bathe in the South Esk River every day. Now, while that river is fine for tossing the odd gun or body into, it is too bloody cold for swimming or washing. But it was fine for tough little Karen.

She got the tattoo of the *Chopper* book cover put on her shoulder, and many a big brave buck in Launceston likes to make smart-arsed comments about it.

Why do these pricks like to say things to a little girl that they would never dream of saying to me? They are weak-gutted mice. The world is full of men who are ready and willing to fight women. They need to be taken to a public toilet and flushed regularly.

In a world of false pretenders and traitors, I have learned to value friendship and loyalty. Karen has those qualities and more. She is more solid than most of the men I know. If she wants to stand on some ratbag's lawn and throw stubbies through his window, then good luck to her. But that, as they say in the classics, is another story.

THE HITCHHIKE QUEEN

They say that sweet ladies who play with knives,
Grow up to become dangerous wives,
I've heard a wild yarn about one man in her life,
Who got it in the back with a Staysharp knife,
Rubbish, she pleaded, it's a lie that gossips tell,
He was drunk and being silly when he slipped and fell,
And although I must confess her story is somewhat shady,
I would never dare question the word of such a lady,
A skinny blonde-haired princess, with eyes of green and grey,
A vampire in the night, a virgin in the day,
Yes, I've known a lot of ladies, from the places I have been,
But none of them quite as crazy as the hitchhike queen,
And her friendship, I must admit, has made me very glad,
So I couldn't care less if she is a little mad.

I am not the only one who finds Karen an attractive item. An old mate, Tony Boros, has given me no peace since he saw her photo in the second book. He was desperate to meet her and offered me a greyhound for her address.

The deal is simple. Karen's full name, address and phone number for the ownership papers for one of his greyhounds. The greyhound gets put in my name and the papers get lodged in Anita's safe. Tony agreed to keep training the dishlicker while I am inside.

I sent someone around to check the dog out and it turned out to be a bloody beauty. So, without bothering to inform the White Dove, I did the deal. Just let's say I like to play Cupid occasionally.

Anyway, that's how I got to own a greyhound. I got a visit from Karen a few days later, asking me who the hell Tony Boros was. It seems he lobbed on her doorstep, sporting a big bunch of flowers and shifty smile. Karen then went on to ask me if I knew anything about a greyhound.

Lucky for me the White Dove has a sense of humour, as not many young ladies would be able to appreciate the comedy involved. I am lucky indeed to have the friendship of such a broadminded lass.

Tony also sent me a photo taken outside Hollywood's famous Chinese Theater. It seems that Humphrey Bogart and me think alike about some things. 'Sid, may you never die till I kill you' signed Humphrey Bogart, 21 August 1946.

I share the sentiment, that's for sure.

As for the White Dove and the greyhound? Well, I guess that blows hell out of my chances of joining the ranks of the sensitive new age guys. Bugger it, who cares? Chicks are beautiful and I would die for them but they are a penny a truckload and a good young greyhound is bloody hard to get hold of.

I mean, let's get things in their right perspective. OK, so I'm not a romantic. But then again, Romeo never owned a greyhound. Ha, ha.

Which brings me back to the romance of Tony and Karen. It was Monday, 9 August when Tony's dreams were to come true. I had the papers for the greyhound and he had my permission to take Karen out for the night of their lives. It was to be the night of passion with the Hillbilly Princess, an evening of romance with the sort of girl a greyhound trainer fantasises about.

When he arrived at the door to pick her up to take her to the Launceston casino, he found that Karen's ex-husband and his mates were in attendance. When Tony walked into the lounge room he said it was like a scene out of the movie *Deliverance*. The only thing missing was the duelling banjos in the background.

There was some wild-looking mountain man chopping wood for the fire - in the lounge room – and some cross-eyed, ill-bred gentleman cleaning a hunting rifle at the kitchen table. Karen's son, a tough toddler named Little Jack, was trying to stab the family pig dog with a fork, much to the animal's understandable annoyance, and White Dove's daughter, Kerrie, was kicking Little Jack in an effort to take the animal's side in the family dispute.

The radio, record player and TV were all blaring away at the same time. It became clear to Tony that this date was not going to be like a scene from a Fred Astaire and Ginger Rogers movie. At that moment Tony started to suspect he may have been stiffed, to give up a perfectly good greyhound for a night out with the passion flower. But it was too late and he had to make the best of it.

The ex-husband was there to look after the kids and Tony and the White Dove made tracks to the casino. Anyway, to cut a long story short, once away from the family anarchy, romance began to blossom and Tony fell deeper under the spell of the beautiful Karen. He then asked her if there was anything she needed. Most girls would ask for a bottle of perfume, or hint that tickets to a rock concert would be nice, maybe even suggest that a diamond ring would woo them, but the White Dove proceeded to put the hard word on him for a truckload of firewood. This was a first for Tony.

The night ended and it came time to hit the bedroom. He found that she slept with a loaded rifle beside the bed. He was advised that it would be best if neither of them went off half-cocked, so to speak.

In spite of everything, romance was in the air and a good time was had by all.

I am left with a problem. Being inside jail, it is difficult to walk my greyhound. The authorities here have been most sympathetic to many of my problems but I think they would baulk at the idea of me popping out of Risdon to walk the favourite for the first leg of the double at the dogs.

I intend to ask Mary-Ann, the babe from the Tax Department, if she would exercise the greyhound for me. The idea of swapping one chick for a greyhound and then getting another to walk it for you strikes me as a classic case of enterprise bargaining at its finest. I am nothing if not an entrepreneur, as many people could tell you.

I have decided to name the greyhound The Buggster, after Damian Bugg, the Director of Public Prosecutions. One must never lose one's sense of humour.

IN LIGHT of these recent events I have decided to rate all females on a one to ten greyhound scale. The White Dove was a one-greyhound girl although I think I got stiffed. Call me old-fashioned, but I would have thought Karen was worth at least two greyhounds. I was new at this trading thing and I will drive harder bargains in future.

I would class Renee Brack as a two-greyhound girl, no problem. Smart, quick and loyal – the greyhounds that is – although there is nothing wrong with Renee that couldn't be fixed quite easily.

The scale is easy: how many greyhounds would the woman in question be worth. Is she a one greyhound girl or is she an Elle MacPherson, who would have to rate nine greyhounds easily? Of course, Ita Buttrose would have to be a 10-greyhound lady, and I'll fight anyone who disagrees.

I do not believe there would be a girl alive worth more than 10 greyhounds. I think this revolutionary greyhound scale would go down well with the down-to-earth, thinking Aussie male. A good dog is worth between $1,000 and $3,000, and never asks for money to go to the hairdressers; you can see that the scale is not as insulting as it may sound.

Personally, I think it is a marvellous idea.

In the midst of all my legal worries I have now got my first vet's bill for The Buggster. He caught some sort of doggie chill and fever and I am now worrying more about the wellbeing of my greyhound than my own problems.

By the look of this bill, if I come back in my next life, it won't be as a gangster. It will be either as a barrister or a vet. Both make more with a pen and a calculator than I ever could with a gun.

If anybody's interested, Tony Boros and Karen ended up going away together for a weekend in Melbourne. Hey, it mightn't be Paris, but it's a step up from chopping wood in the lounge room.

Those two are having a lovely time while The Buggster still requires medical attention. By the time he is well enough to race he will have had more jabs in the bum than a Filipino bar girl …

HAVING finally got over the doggie 'flu, The Buggster was ready to show a select few how quick he was. But the big deal greyhound blew his monkey muscle at the time trials. He ran a swift 26.1 seconds, then he did this small muscle in his back. The vet bills aren't worth it.

My sense of humour is no longer with me and a greyhound with a dodgy back is the last thing. Maybe we could get it on Workcare and live off the pension for a few years. But then again, maybe not. And so there is a better than even money chance that he could end up as Number 27 on the menu of the local Vietnamese restaurant.

Between verballing bikies, hillbilly blondes, dodgy greyhounds and lovestruck tax inspectors, my cup runneth over. I am fast turning into a mental paralytic.

I need help … and a canine chiropractor.

SADLY, I have been told that, while Karen and Tony go from strength to strength, The Buggster is no more. Here in Tassie, slow greyhounds are a penny a truckload and no one wants one with a dodgy monkey muscle. Apparently after the trial it pulled up shaking and had a little bark (a vomit, not a woof). It was decided, without consulting me, I may add, to put the thing out of its misery.

They shot the bloody thing.

I only hope Sid Collins pulls a monkey muscle one day.

THE GREYHOUND QUESTION

In the games played between men and women,
The greyhound has its place,
The two have a lot in common,
Pet them right and they'll both lick your face,
Would you swap your lady for a greyhound?
Would you ask for two or maybe three?
Speaking for myself, two's OK by me,
Three greyhounds for your sister?
And your mother? Maybe four?
And if you really love your wife,
You're allowed to ask for more,
It's a social question that presents us with a puzzle:
One wears lipstick; the other wears a muzzle.
So remember next time you come home late,
And she's tossed your dinner on the floor,
Just tell her you'll swap her for a greyhound,
Let's face it …
She can't be worth much more.

Ha ha.

CHAPTER 8

PRUNING WITH DAVE

'THE STONE-KILLING RATBAG
COULD TAKE A TURN FOR THE WORSE,
REAL QUICK, SO I LET HIM GO'

One of Read's best friends is a former Melbourne private schoolboy from a privileged background. A non-drinker, non-smoker known only as 'Dave the Jew', he was Read's partner on several abductions and murders. He is 'as smart as a whip and as dangerous as a black snake on a dark night', according to Read. Tasmanian police were concerned that Dave, a master of disguise, may try to kill prosecution witnesses who were prepared to testify against Read. The Jew may well be mentally disturbed but, according to Chopper, a good man to have on your side.

WHEN you're in the business of standing over people and being a criminal garbage collector you soon learn that some jobs are easy and some a little harder. There was one toe-cutting operation which certainly had its problems and I still shudder when I think back.

Dave the Jew was in charge of proceedings and insisted on using a pair of old garden secateurs instead of boltcutters or the trusty gas bottle. I always liked the bottle because the victim would often talk when he saw the flame had been lit and he knew he would be first course in a little barbeque.

But Dave didn't like the gas. He said it gave him a headache and that the fumes and the smell made his eyes water and his nose run.

'Nonsense,' I told him. But Dave always enjoyed complaining and arguing the point and because I was such a good-natured chap I nearly always let him have his way.

'Very well, use the clippers,' I said. Dave didn't need a second invitation. I took no part in the interrogation. 'All this fuss over a mere 26 grand,' I said to the gentleman concerned at the time. He did not answer, for he was trussed like a Christmas turkey at that moment.

Dave then beat the fellow from neck to knee with a length of iron pipe that must have broken half the bones in his body. We were in the keg cellar of a mate's pub. It was a quiet, dark place that suited our need for privacy.

The bloke had already told us where to find his stash and we had sent a helper, a chap who helped Dave the Jew out now and again, to get the money. The old guy, named Kevin, was an eager helper and he raced out to the house to search for the cash. Our target was in no position to go out to point out where the money was hidden.

But Kevin was up to the task, and two hours later came back with $25,000 plus a little bonus, the victim's E Type Jag, a white, low-slung beauty that was in perfect condition. I would have loved to have kept it, but I knew it would lead the heat to us and was too risky. I told Kevin to take it back.

It looked like a clean win for us. We had the cash, the car was on the way back and all that was needed was for me to tie up a few loose ends.

I pulled out my gun and was about to pop a slug into the eyeball of the hoon we were dealing with when Dave said: 'No, no, no, this one is mine.'

It was no big deal to me, so I sat back down, cracked a cold can and munched away on a family-size pizza that Kevin had brought back with him.

Dave wanted to cut the poor bugger's toes off, just to see how effective the garden secateurs were for the job. I was not happy with this and told Dave this sort of thing was not called for. But Dave argued that it would not worry the victim because he had already snapped the guy's spine during the beating with the iron pipe.

As if to prove his rather gruesome point, Dave popped off one of the toes on the victim's left foot and, sure enough, the bloke just lay there, he didn't even let out a whimper. He obviously didn't feel a thing.

I still feel ill at ease about the propriety of Dave's conduct, but I knew better than to argue with the Jew when he was in the grip of blood lust. The stone-killing ratbag could take a turn for the worse, real quick, so I let him go. I got up and checked the victim who, for the sake of the story, we will call Angelo. He was looking very dopey and glassy-eyed to me, but he had a strong pulse. My blood pressure pumps along at 105 over 68 and Angelo's was 140 over 90, a bit higher than my own, but doing very nicely considering he was half dead.

Whenever I checked the blood pressure and pulse of a man about to die or someone we were questioning, Dave would laugh and say: 'Look at Doctor Chopper.' But I like to check these things as a matter of routine. Dave popped off one of Angelo's big toes and it flew across the floor and out of sight between some kegs.

It was all getting quite sickening. Kevin returned, having taken Angelo's Jag back where it belonged. He wondered why Angelo was still alive. 'Dave's in one of his experimental medical moods,' I said.

Dave lost his temper. 'Don't ever say that,' he said. 'He's in no pain at all.'

'You're a raving nut case,' I yelled back. 'Kill the poor bastard.'

'No,' cried the Jew. 'He's in no pain.'

'I'll kill him,' said Kevin. We both looked at Kevin. The evil old toe-cutter had killed his fair share before, but this was none of his business. Then for some reason we all looked down and Angelo was crying, bloody crying.

'Now look what you've done,' yelled Dave.

I've seen them cry before, but this was different, he was crying sad silent tears. It was then that I started to feel a little sorry for him. 'For God's sake Dave, just finish it,' I pleaded. Dave must have also felt bad, as he did what I asked, thank God. It was a very bad job, messy and all over the shop. We whacked the dough up. It was 10 grand each for Dave and me and around five for old Kevin. For his money, Kevin had to clean up and get rid of the body.

Torturing them and killing them is easy. Getting rid of the remains is the worst job of all. Neither Dave nor I like that part of the job and we felt we were toe-cutting toffs, top of the head-hunting hierarchy, and above that sort of work. When we could off-load the dirty work on a helper, we were quick to do so. But as a rule, we got stuck with that job as well. It is the lowest job of all, cleaning up and getting rid of the mortal remains.

But this time, old Kevin was made to earn his $5,000 by doing the dirty work. I thought we had left the job in good hands, but a week later I got a call from my mate who owned the pub complaining of the stink from his keg cellar.

As soon as I went down there I smelled a rat, or worse. The place looked clean and you could smell disinfectant, but you could also smell rotting flesh.

I told my mate to go back upstairs and I stayed in the cellar and pulled the kegs out searching for what I knew was the offending item. It was the big toe that Dave had cut off. After about 30 minutes I found it. Bloody hell, a week-old toe is not a pretty sight. I have heard of green thumbs but green toes are something altogether different. I went upstairs and flushed it down the toilet. I washed the cellar down and told my mate to leave the trap door open overnight to get rid of the stench.

Dave the Jew was not pleased at the news and old Kevin, who had been cutting toes with Jimmy the Porn in the late 1960s, and was an old hand, was most sorry. Dave nearly shot the old fellow, but all was well in the end.

The whole job stuck in my memory as a bad luck job. Angelo's tears did not sit well with me. It was the last time I allowed the Jew to take control of matters. Left in charge he could be a total butcher.

There have been very few violent Jewish criminals in Australia, but violent Jews carved themselves a large slice of the American organised crime scene, and earned themselves a bloody and violent reputation.

Dave the Jew is a violent, bloody, smiling, polite, well-mannered, educated, polished, shy, cultured, head-hunting, toe-cutting, stone-killing, psychopathic rattlesnake, who would be more at home in the mean streets of New York than the quiet avenues of Melbourne.

Dave often told me about his Uncle Benny, who died in a gun battle with a gang of Italians in Brooklyn's lower east side. Dave said his uncle, known as 'Benny Blue Eyes', was part of a Jewish gang which teamed up with a mad Irish crew to fight the Italians. Uncle Benny ran three blocks with four slugs in him before he fell down dead. In the shoot-out, six people were killed: three Italians, two Irish and Benny. It took place in 1932 and Uncle Benny was only 15 years old. Naturally, Dave only ever heard his family's side of the story and this gave him a hatred for Italians.

Another family legend which made Dave hate Italians concerned another relative who was stabbed in the chest with a bayonet while being pushed into a freight car of a train bound for Germany. Dave was told the offender in this case was an Italian soldier. The relative was a girl just 12 years old, his mother's cousin. This along with other various horror stories from the war about relatives being whacked out in various death camps really stuck with old Dave.

'The Germans,' he said, 'were monsters. But at least they were honest monsters. But the treachery of the Italians and the French and their treatment of the Jews cannot be forgiven or forgotten.'

And let me tell you, Dave has a long memory. One thing he taught me about the Jewish revenge mentality is that the sins of the father will fall on the heads of the sons, or grandsons, or great grandsons, and so on. They forget nothing and forgive nothing.

Dave hates Italians because a Dago shot his uncle in 1932 and an Italian soldier bayoneted his mother's cousin in World War II … so you can imagine his reaction whenever we grab an Italian for some toe-cutting work.

The bloke is a raving nut case, but I love him, bless his insane heart.

IN THE early 1970s the bashing of poofs along the Yarra River walkway and in the Fitzroy Gardens, to name a couple of places, was considered not just the done thing, but the height of good humour. Cowboy Johnny was a great one for this before I met him and tried hard to encourage the Surrey Road Gang to join these after dark recreational pursuits. But Dave the Jew, ever the toff, thought such activities vulgar and uncouth. Dave was, and still is, a criminal snob, much like my good self, and didn't want to soil his hands flogging poo pushers in public dunnies.

Terry the Tank was neither here nor there on the issue, happy to go along with whatever I decided. The Cowboy felt that we should have a meeting on the matter and a vote, so under the stage of the Try Boys' Youth Club, a gang meeting was held. I was the General, but Dave the Jew was a nutter who carried a loaded .38 calibre handgun on him at all times. So let's just say I was not a foolish General.

I explained that as leader of the gang I would remain neutral and go along with what the three of them wanted. 'Well, I reckon we should bash the shirt lifters,' said the Cowboy. Terry the Tank kept silent, sensing a showdown between the Jew and the Cowboy. The Jew spoke: 'I for one will not be hunting through the public lavatories of this city in search of pansies.'

The Cowboy, sensing a highbrow debate for which he was

obviously ill-equipped, used a basic psychological trick to try to grab the high ground. 'Are you a poof then?' the Cowboy sneered.

Even I would never have spoken to the Jew in such a manner. The Jew was livid. 'I will not be bullied into bashing poofs. I am not a poof and if you weren't a mental defective I'd shoot you,' he said to the Cowboy.

Crash! Dave hit the deck and the Cowboy started throwing punches. No one called Cowboy Johnny Harris a 'mental detective'. That's what the poor old Cowboy thought the Jew had called him, a mental detective, and the poor, simple Cowboy thought the Jew had accused him of being some sort of mad policeman. The truth was that me, the Jew and Terry the Tank wouldn't have beaten the Cowboy in a fist fight even if we attacked him when he was asleep. We beat Johnny via the use of friendship and mind control. The Jew was in big trouble, he was being punched stupid. I yelled to Terry to break it up. Terry the Tank rushed in, only to be punched to the floor in half a second by the Cowboy, who had got his second wind.

I screamed to the Cowboy to stop it at once and to cut it out. He paused for long enough for me to rush in and grab Dave's handgun out of his coat before the Jew could regain his wits.

After a while Dave and Terry regained their senses, if that was at all possible, and I laid down the law. 'Right,' I said. 'We are going out right now to bash a few poofs and that is all there is to it.' I gave Dave back his gun, after removing all the bullets.

Dave said, 'All right, but I go under protest.' But first Johnny wanted Dave to say sorry for calling him a mental detective. 'Defective,' said Dave. 'Defective, not detective.'

Cowboy looked puzzled and said, 'What's a defective'. Dave just smiled, shook his head and put his hand on Cowboy's shoulder and said, 'I rest my case.' So, laughing, but with Cowboy still a wee bit confused, we went off in search of bottom bandits.

We headed straight for the Fawkner Park toilets, which were

infamous for unwholesome nocturnal activities, but believe it or not, we couldn't even find the toilets. 'This is insanity,' said Dave. 'We can't even find the dyke, let alone the bloody poofs.'

So we took a tram to St Kilda, got off and walked to the Lower Esplanade, where there was a public toilet block which was supposed to be the gay boys' version of heaven. It was a famous hang out (literally) for shirt lifters and pillow biters. It was homosexual HQ.

So there we were, hanging about outside the dunnies without a lot happening. We decided that Terry the Tank, Cowboy and I should hide and leave Dave out the front as bait for the gay boys. After about five minutes a police car pulled up and both coppers got out to question Dave. They ordered him to move on or they would charge him with loitering for the purposes of soliciting. They were convinced that Dave was a poof hanging about for a quickie. After the police car cleared off, we came back to find Dave bright red. He was livid.

'They thought I was a poof,' yelled an outraged Dave. He was very upset. It was not his night, and our laughter did not help matters.

We went back to Fawkner Park and this time I was the bait. Thank God it was dark. A la-de-da gentleman minced up to me and asked me the time. I told him I didn't have a watch. He then asked me, 'How big is your lunch box?' I just stood there because I didn't understand poof slang. Dave then yelled out from his hiding spot that the guy was a poof. The gent, then realising the game at hand, decided to move along with some haste. Dave took off after him, with gun in hand. Then 'bang, bang' and we saw two bright muzzle flashes in the dark. I don't know who was more shocked – me or the poof. I had taken all Dave's ammo, but the shifty bugger always carried another six rounds in his pocket, as I was later to learn.

The poof took off, with Dave running after him. Then the bloke fell over and Dave was on him, pistol whipping the poor bastard. The police accusing Dave of being a faggot had turned our minority-loving, articulate friend into a homophobic madman, out for blood. We had created a monster.

The three of us had to drag the Jew off this half-dead poof. From then on, we had to keep an eye on Dave, and keep him away from homosexual areas. He was a stone killer, and could not be trifled with. He didn't want to beat up poofs for fun, he wanted to kill them, all because two policemen in St Kilda had thought he was queer.

It was some time before Dave got over his homophobic condition. But even today, I would fear for the life of any misguided gay gent who made himself known to the Jew, with any rude offers.

Dave had an upper-class refined manner and an educated, private school, speaking voice, which he sometimes tries to disguise with an Aussie-style slang tone. Dave thinks his educated voice made the police think he was of the limp-wristed persuasion. It gave the Jew quite a psychological complex. Our adventure into the world of poof bashing sent an already mentally distressed Jew into the world of even deeper insanity.

Poor Dave. Ha ha.

> *Ziggy's gone, now vanished and very dead,*
> *Dave did the job, and whacked one in his head,*
> *Ziggy was a wise guy, a drug land fixer,*
> *But he got laid to rest, with a pink cement mixer,*
> *It took two goes to get him, the first one was a joke,*
> *Dave got the wrong address, and clipped the wrong bloke.*

CHAPTER 9

KLAN FAN MAIL

'DANE AND HIS ILK ARE DITHERING,
EFFEMINATE DRAMA QUEENS, GADDING
ABOUT LIKE A HIGH-CAMP NAZI VERSION
OF THE VILLAGE PEOPLE'

IN READ'S second book, he discussed the growing trend in Australian jails for criminals to align themselves with bizarre cults and groups, including ultra-Right Wing factions such as the Nazis and the Ku Klux Klan. He wrote at length of convicted murderer Dane Sweetman, a self-confessed Nazi and skinhead. Read described Sweetman as a lightweight and suggested that in World War II, Himmler might well have placed Sweetman in a specimen jar and displayed him in the Heidelberg University. He also discussed Sweetman's wedding, in H Division, to his long-time girlfriend, Lynwen. The couple were married in traditional skinhead gear.

Sweetman was not impressed with Read's irreverent thoughts about National Socialism and other matters. He asked for, and was given, the right of reply.

Sweetman was sentenced to 20 years' jail for the murder of David Noble in April 1990. The Supreme Court was told that he and another man were celebrating Adolf Hitler's birthday when they killed Noble. Sweetman is not eligible for parole until 18 November 2005.

I RECEIVE a steady flow of hate mail, most of it boring, humdrum, predictable, a total yawn, unsigned, with no return address, and calling me every foul name under the sun. All of it goes into the bin. But when I got a lovely letter from Dane Sweetman in Pentridge, I decided it had to see the light of day.

It was so well written that it obviously took him a long time to put together. He has abused me in such an upmarket manner, never at any stage lowering himself to cheap insults, that you'd hardly guess his lips move as he reads and writes. In fact, as far as hate mail goes, it is quite highbrow, even state of the art. Anyway, I enjoyed reading it so much I thought I might share it with the public. It is only fair that I give a member of the Chopper Read Hate Club a fair hearing and right of reply, because at least he had the honesty to sign it. Dave the Jew told me that his old Hebrew teacher was a Rabbi named Sweetman and Dave's dad said with a name like Sweetman Dane should call himself the Yom Kippur Nazi.

Spectators don't win wars and in my view Dane and his ilk are dithering, effeminate drama queens, gadding about like a high-camp Nazi version of the Village People. Dangerous, by all means, but an embarrassment, not only to themselves but also to anyone who views them, parading around in their Nazi gay gear, with a collective bloodline as pure as Himmler's porridge.

What the modern Nazi movement forgets is that the Jews of today, the Israelis, had the best teacher of all time, Adolf Hitler. Having survived the fires of Hitler, it is laughable to think that the Jewish race will fall into a screaming heap at the hands of Neo-Nazi gay boy false pretenders.

Your worst enemy is your best teacher and, after Adolf, anything else is a walk in the park. Dream on, Dane, because that's all you've got. Seig Heil.

P.S. I sent Dane a short letter of reply advising him not to lose his sense of humour and wishing him a happy Rosh Hashanah, the Jewish New Year. Ha ha ha.

To Mark B Read
C/O Risdon Prison
Tasmania
Australia

Heil Hitler

Mark, I am not in the habit of casting aspersions upon any man, but you fall into the category of highly exceptional. Your pejorative comments and infantile attempts to parody myself and my creed fell severely short and are nothing more than insane.

You are a literal parasite of shallow and predictable character and, not forgetting, critically superficial intelligence. Your quaint little books have become somewhat of a Leviathan, but still one could blindly read the inspired garbage you have ejaculated down the throats of the gullible collective masses. Myself, like so many, have suffered dysentery upon reading your interminable maelstrom of the laymanly perverse.

You are, in all facets of character, very naïve, conceited and egocentric and last, but not least, a well-versed advocate of your dullard psyche egotism. You attack on the moronic asinine plane, influencing every misanthrope and every lecherous type, thus, ipso facto, you cannot help yourself. You are a recidivist, even in literature.

I am incensed that I had the misfortune of ever meeting you and do not envy those who have. You lack the capacity to write anything of valued taste. But this is of no wonder. You are ignoble, which accounts for your pretentiousness.

How insidious of you to question my intelligence

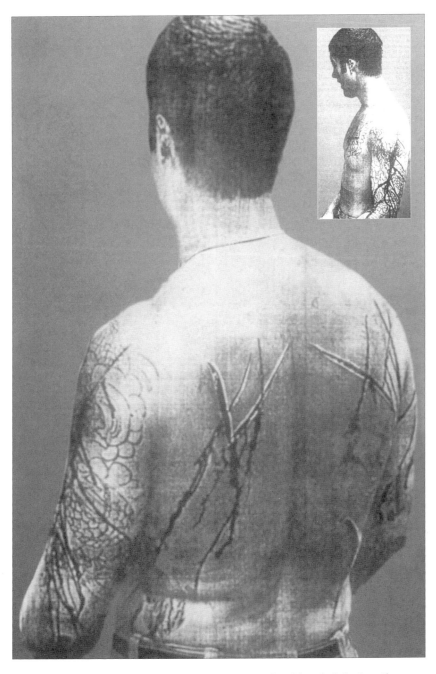

Ouch! These were taken in Pentridge prison soon after I handed the late Jimmy Loughnan a razor in 1978.

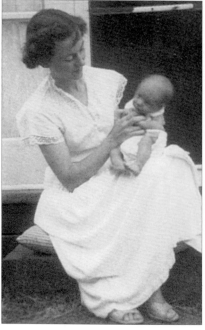

I must have been a beautiful baby …

… but look at me now!

Damian Bugg, QC. He ain't never chased a rabbit …

Above: ... not to be confused with The Buggster, who was too slow to catch any.

Below: Tony Boros in Melbourne with the White Dove for a romantic weekend. I swapped her address for a greyhound.

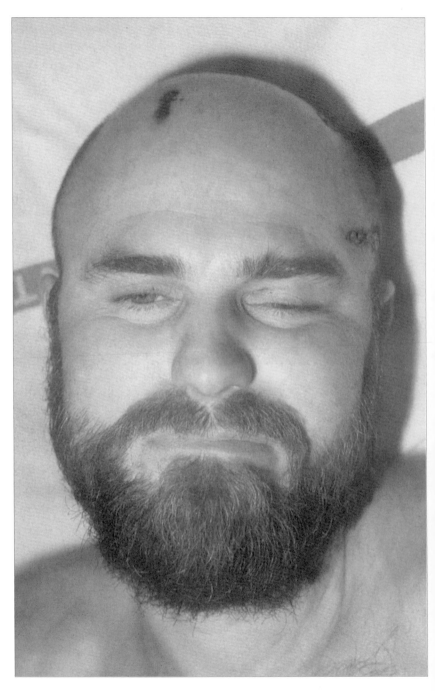

Pavel 'Mad Max' Marinof on the slab after being shot dead by police. Good shot …

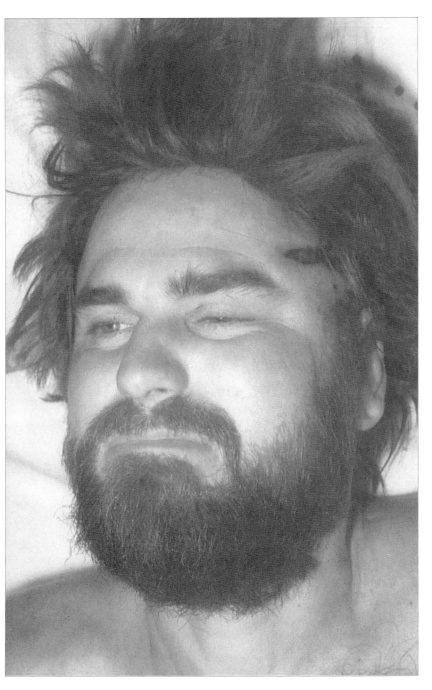

… bad rug.

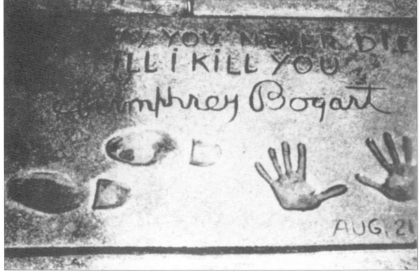

Above: Dad – loyal to the last.

Below: Bogey and I agree.

and insolently denounce the White Aryan Cause. You profess to know so much, but all you are is a thoughtless plagiarist, a thief, a ravenous predator who is running short of founded and established clichés and the raw sewage you sprout in your rancid excuse for tolerable reading.

For someone who has only met me once, you have a high perception of my activity. I have never used drugs in my life, not intentionally, and am vexed beyond comprehension that you cite this vicious lie.

You made parody of my marriage. Reference to my wife's attire and mine was totally facetious. I just happen to love and revere my wife for her stalwart commitment and 15 years service to National Socialism and the inexorable quest for skinhead unity. Where you confuse love with the lecherous bastardizing way of the cantankerous Jew and Nigger, I fortunately do not. I would never demean the woman I profess to love so blatantly by baring her arse for the whole race-diseased country to lovingly visualize. Have you no shame or thought for your woman's virtue?

You are about as Right-Wing as Humphrey B. Bear and you shall aspire to nothing more than a festering pile on the vulnerable arse of the White Aryan humanity.

You are the victim of your own zealous aspirations and insecurities. Your pathos is sickening.

As for your satirical quip about the bleeding heart liberals and gay commies, I do not have to explain myself to you, but I am as intellectual as anyone and any revisionist well versed in National Socialism as a way of social strength and living, Adolf Hitler and all wars from the first Saxon invasion in 747 AD. I welcome any political or historical challenge put forward to try and thwart the Fuhrer's truth.

Adolf Hitler is right. 'If you cut even cautiously into such an abscess you've found like a maggot in a rotting corpse often dazzled by a sudden light, a Kike.'

Your books are an abscess and you are of equivocal race.

Your beration upon me has done the cause more good than intended detriment. Any publicity, no matter how subversive, highlights our Fuhrer's bequeathment a thousandfold.

And there is nothing Neo about us of the ANM. We were nurtured by the greatest strategic genius that ever lived, Adolf Hitler.

Cell Leader A.N.M. Victoria
Mr Dane Sweetman
ANM 2752
Guard Leader PMKKK

CHAPTER 10

JAILHOUSE BLUES

'THE GENERAL PUBLIC SCREAMS FOR THE
BLOOD OF CHILD KILLERS AND CHILD SEX
OFFENDERS, BUT WHEN CHOPPER READ
BASHES OR STABS ONE OF THESE VERMIN,
THE COURTS TURN ON ME AND CALL ME A
DANGER TO THE PUBLIC'

THE best jailhouse lawyer in any prison in Australia is a man from one of the biggest crime families in the country.

Mind you, the rest of his relatives make the Addams Family look like the Brady Bunch. They are a collection of police informers, old bags and toothless, tattooed, brain-dead, gutless, limp-wristed morons, and that's the best half of the family tree. Of the whole mob, the jailhouse lawyer is the brightest spark indeed. He got involved in drugs and crimes of violence. If he had been brought up in the right family he could have been a brilliant lawyer rather than a drug dealer. Of course, some would say the morals of both trades are roughly the same.

He is a man who has studied law while in jail and, when he is not moving drugs, spends his time learning about legal history.

He told me once about a famous case in London, at the Old Bailey, where there was a very old judge, believed to be well over 90.

It was an important case, because it made the British legal world question how old a judge should be allowed to be before his judgement may be called into question.

This old fellow was well known for falling asleep during trials, and then waking up with a jolt, not really knowing what case was before him.

This time he was sitting, or sleeping, through a murder trial. A farmer from Kent had been charged with killing his good lady wife. He had been accused of strangling his wife and tossing the body down the well. The wife's pet name was Pussy. The case dragged on and the details unfolded slowly. The old judge began to take short naps, with his head nodding forward. Back in those days no prosecutor would dare declare the old fool was asleep. The trick was simply to raise your voice and hope he was a light sleeper. That way you had a chance of waking up the napping judge – and maybe startle a couple of members of the jury before they nodded off as well.

The farmer was being cross-examined, and the prosecutor loudly accused him of brutally strangling his dear wife and then tossing the poor woman down the well.

The old judge awoke with a jolt and began laughing. He then said, 'Ho, ho, ho. No doubt a case of ding dong dell, Pussy's in the well.'

The whole courtroom erupted in uncontrolled laughter with the old judge absolutely delighted with his quick wit. He was so chuffed that he cried out again: 'Ding dong dell, Pussy's in the well.'

It was all too much for the prosecutor, especially when the old judge nodded off half way through his own summing up.

It is a funny story, but the point is that not a real lot has changed. Judges live in a small world of their own. They live a sheltered life, a life of privileged advantage. They have a certain immunity, they are waited on, protected, and what most of them know about the real world is limited indeed.

Yes, there are some notable exceptions to the rule, but most judges know an enormous amount about the law, and bugger-all about real life.

They are, in short, a most stupid breed.

Many I have struck (I wish literally) have proved ignorant,

overbearing, ill-informed, presumptuous, flatulent arseholes, and that's only their good points.

One is forced to question the sexual likes and dislikes of some of them. After all, they are in a job where it is perfectly normal to wear a dress and a funny wig during working hours. One has to wonder what they do for kicks afterwards.

When will judges wake up and start to consider the victim? Oh, that's right, they do consider the victim in certain circumstances. Frighten a bank teller with a shotgun and you'll get 15 years; frighten a six-year-old girl by involving her in some sexual perversion, 15 months. Bash a full-grown gangster and you'll get four or five years; bash the crap out a child and you'll get four or five months, plus free visits to a shrink.

If judges refuse to protect children, why should they be treated with respect? There are exceptions, but most judges are a total waste of public money. On the whole, they are a collection of fluffy ducks who can't find the pond.

I remember one time when I was waiting to be sentenced. In the next cell was some piece of vermin who had been having sex with his two daughters and bringing home other men to do the same. He was charging them money to screw his little girls. They were aged nine and ten. It had been going on since they were about six.

I was there because I had shot some chap who had put a hole in his manners. I got two years. The other fellow got a bond and was ordered to undergo medical treatment. I would have liked to give him some medical treatment, with a meat cleaver.

The judges have it wrong. They are outraged when one crim shoots another, but when the deviants have their way with unsuspecting children, they get a 12-month bond. The next thing they will be handing out medals for perversion.

As far as I am concerned, the rape of a child should be punished twice as hard as the rape of a woman. If a violent sex attack can upset the mental and emotional wellbeing of a woman, the mind boggles at what it must do to a child.

Any judge who can look the world in the eye after letting a child sex attacker off with a bond or a 12-month sentence is, in my opinion, a party to that crime and should be spat on in the street.

I have jammed broom handles up the bums of child sex attackers in jail. I have kicked the scum near to death and I have been punished for it and called a monster, but the judges who refuse to protect the little children are the real perverted monsters.

I spit on them all.

I HAVE been described as a monster, but what sort of monster am I supposed to be?

I am a monster who has never hurt a woman, a child or an old person. The general public screams for the blood of child killers and child sex offenders, but when Chopper Read bashes or stabs one of these vermin, the courts turn on me and call me a danger to the public.

The general public screams for the blood of drug dealers, but when I put a blow torch to the feet of a few drug peddlers, and shoot a few more, the courts declare me the dangerous one.

I am a monster who has not turned his hand to an innocent member of the general public, except for the time I attacked Judge Martin, and even then we ended up writing to each other. He forgave me for what I did and I still feel bad about it.

The courts say that the people I have hurt are members of the public and should be protected. Hang on, I thought the public was meant to be protected from sex offenders and drug pushers. Yet, when I spill a little of their blood, suddenly this lot of vermin are promoted to general public class. Are members of the criminal underworld really members of the general public? Should they be protected? Do they deserve the same rights as the rest of the community? Or is the truth that they have chosen a path in a dog-eat-dog world, so they should cop what they get and not whinge about it?

Justice Cox, in Tassie, said that it appeared that all my violence had been directed towards members of the criminal underworld, then declared me a danger to the general public.

Now, call me a social buffoon, but what is what and who is whom? A drug dealer is either an enemy of the public or a member of the public. He cannot be both. The whole argument is nonsensical to me. I am 'a danger to the public' because I have shot, killed and tortured a few members of the criminal world.

If that's not Irish logic, I'm a Dutchman. You may as well charge rat catchers with being kidnappers as far as I'm concerned.

CHAPTER 11

WHY GOD INVENTED RAZOR BLADES

'YOU ARE NOT A COWARD BECAUSE
YOU FEEL FEAR. IT IS THERE TO STOP US
TONGUE-KISSING TIGER SNAKES'

FRANKIE Waghorn's mum rang Margaret with the terrible 'news' that I had been bashed in Risdon Prison. This is about the 20th time I've been the alleged victim of violence most foul behind the walls of the Pink Palace.

Ages ago, Anita Betts came to me most concerned over reports that I was being picked on by the bigger boys. I was even the victim of a stabbing in my cell, according to one wild story. I was the unlucky victim of a kicking attack, and I've had my head punched in so many times that I would get a thick ear, if I had one left, just listening to it all. How these wild rumours and stories start I do not know. But I seem to be the sad victim of all these fantasy attacks. I wish the numb nuts who think up all this rubbish would let me win one or two. According to the gossip and rumour mongers, I haven't won a single round. Is this a psychological campaign to talk me to death? Is it all a case of wishful thinking, or do people have such a good time thinking all this sort of crap up?

I go out of my way to avoid three things: manual labour, physical exercise and fisticuffs. While others engage in all manner of combat training, pumping iron, punching bags, kicking each other, huffing and puffing and sweating like pigs in an effort to build themselves into fighting machines, I prefer to avoid all that hard work.

I do all my fighting with a gun in one hand and a cup of tea in the other. While the world is full of people who could bash me, the world is not full of people who could bash me and live to talk about it. That's why God invented razor blades, butcher's knives, iron bars, meat axes and guns that go bang – so blokes like me don't get bashed 10 times a day before breakfast.

If people want to try and bash me that's fine, as long as they don't mind spending the rest of their lives in a wheelchair or being led around by a seeing-eye dog.

If they really want to rock and roll, then it would be a coffin for them. The only thing I get bashed with these days is bullshit. Shoot me, but for goodness sake, don't shit me, as the old saying goes.

There have been many and various rumours floating around Tassie and it would appear they are never complete unless they include my good self. I heard that I was filthy rich from money from book sales. I just wish it was true. I was supposed to have bought Anita a new car from the proceeds. Fat chance. She already drives a Mercedes. The book wouldn't have paid for one back wheel.

One great local rumour was that I had put out a $20,000 contract on the life of Trent Anthony, fetch and carry boy and general lackey turned Crown witness.

Naturally, Micky Marlow had his name thrown into the ruck

The CIB questioned a bloke by the name of Dennis Carr over the matter. It was rumoured that young Dennis, an alleged criminal identity in Tasmania, was seen parked outside a police safehouse with another gent who looked a little like old Mad Micky. Dennis told me this wild story when he popped into the remand yard, before getting appeal bail over a small matter.

It seems the police are prepared to believe the wildest yarns where my name is concerned.

I guess my Crown witnesses, God bless them, will be seeing hitmen in their dreams for years to come, and the police will believe any dreamer with a good Chopper Read yarn to tell.

Ha ha.

HEROIN seems to have a worse effect on ladies than on men. It will drive a man to crime, but it seems to take women's souls. It sends them to the streets and the parlours. Women are not very good at armed robbery and violent crime, and the quickest and simplest way to pay the bills and support their drug habits is to lay on their backs with their legs open.

Not all ladies in this area and in that life with a drug habit are lost souls. I have seen a few dive head first into it, swim around for several years and then I have seen them years later, alive and well, healthy and happy.

They have danced with the devil and escaped by some freak or fluke. Maybe they were stronger than smack, but the few who have pulled themselves out of it are rare indeed. The love of a child can do it, or sometimes the love of a man. Love seems to be the magic that has saved them. I have seen others give away the world for heroin when they seemed to have everything on their side.

I don't know the answer. I have seen some escape, but most go under. Those who have survived are the freaky few.

I'D LIKE to clear up one point, if I may. I get mail from some people who see me as some sort of Robin Hood, a crusader who has set himself up to clean the world of drug dealers. I am not an avenging angel and I do not see myself as one.

There are two main reasons why I target drug dealers. First, they are the ones with the big money. One is hardly going to make a big profit from kidnapping and torturing men who pinch washing machines for a living, so it's simply a matter of logical economics. Secondly, a drug dealer is in no position to tell on you, that is, if he lives to tell any tales at all. The general public does not give a toss what happens to drug dealers, fair or foul.

Judges take a dim view of it but juries, as a rule, are far more sympathetic.

I don't want people to get the wrong impression. I don't take from the rich and give to the poor. I keep the money myself. My life will never be made into a Disney movie. I don't like drug dealers, that much is true, but it is really beside the point.

It is business. It is not and has never been some sort of holy crusade. But it can be fun, and quite profitable too.

A STORY of death and violence was told to me by my old friend Vincent Villeroy. A good bedtime story for the kiddies – if you want them to grow up to be psychos.

Vincent was part of a crew who grabbed a payroll bandit. They cut off his toes with a pair of hedge clippers, just as a warm up, and when the poor fellow later asked who was torturing him, Vincent told him not to be so nosy. Ha ha.

They kept hitting him with a cattle prod by pushing it into his nose and giving him a zap with the electric volts which went straight into his brain.

Vincent and his mates kicked a big goal with that one. There was only $30,000 involved and it was hard to go four ways.

They disposed of the body by chopping it up and feeding it to the pigs. I always think of it when I have an egg and bacon sandwich.

Getting animals to eat the remains of a murder victim is a good trick. Pigs are great and chickens are wonderful. I have known chaps to go through the chain feeder on a chicken farm. It not only gets rid of the evidence, but makes the yolks nice and yellow.

In Tassie, there is no need to use domestic animals as accessories after the fact. Just leave the body in the bush and the Tasmanian devils will do the rest. They have extra strong jaws for crunching bones. They feed in packs and will eat anything at all, a bit like armed robbery squad detectives. Wonderful.

KYM Nelson was a well-known lady in the Melbourne criminal world during the '60s, '70s and even the '80s. Kym was a top-looking lady in her day, smart and tough to go with it. She was a gangster's girl with boyfriends like Joey Hamilton and old-time gangsters like Bertie Kidd, to name a few. Tracy Warren used to work for her. I was too polite to ask what Tracy did, but no doubt it was something in the public relations field.

A famous feud broke out between Kym and old Granny Evil herself – the old bat who gave birth to the greatest group of creeps, no hopers and police informers in Victoria's history. Granny Evil was one of the biggest figures in the crime world and she didn't like Kym at all.

Anyway, one day the old whore went to see Kym, taking her number one son along for the ride. But they didn't see eye to eye about things, no pun intended. Whatever happened that day, the old bag had her eye shot out and Kym lived to fight another day.

Naturally, I have no idea what happened that day, although the old bitch in question has always remained rather one-eyed about her opinion of Kym.

I saw the whole fiasco as the very height of good humour and rolled around the floor laughing when I heard. Kym was one tough chick that the family couldn't kill. Nevertheless, she would be well advised to keep an eye out for them.

The police had a secret operation into the old one-eyed bag and her family. They called it Cyclops. Who said coppers didn't have a sense of humour? The old woman had such a full life they should make a movie about her, and call it 'For Your Eye Only'.

AS OUR friends in the Mafia movies are fond of saying, business is business and it is not personal. That is my motto regarding any act of violence. Once you start to take these things personally, that is when you will lose the game.

If you are motivated through anger, grief, fear or any other emotion, you have lost the edge and that is the touch which makes the difference. It is a cool head, not hot blood, that makes the best people in the business of death.

I always look at it this way: once he is dead, he won't remember the pain. So in the scheme of things, it doesn't matter, does it? The pain is only business and the death is the end of pain. Business, then business is over. Quite simple.

Anita Betts asked me why I seemed so calm and totally without anger when I was found guilty of the Sid Collins matter. She wanted to know why I remained so peaceful when the judge announced that I was sentenced to Governor's Pleasure. It was because it was only business.

Instead of ranting and raving, rolling about and sooking at the injustice of it all, I simply look at this way: it is never checkmate until I'm dead; until then, it is just another move on the board.

They make their move, I make mine. I don't take it personally and I hope they don't either.

By getting angry I would lose my edge. Wars are won by men who are willing to fight them for a long time.

WHEN I look back on the jelly beans I have shot, stabbed, bashed, iron-barred, axed, knee-capped, toe-cut, blowtorched, killed and generally up-ended, I look at it like this: if I hadn't done it, then somebody else would have. I am not the only lion in the jungle, but I am the only one with no ears and a smiling face.

Believe it or not, I have retired, but it doesn't mean I have changed. When I get out, and get out I will, I will still have my guns. People might think that because I will have guns I won't have left the crime world. That is not true – it's just that I don't want to leave this mortal world just yet awhile.

I have too many enemies ever to just relax. I have gone too far to turn the clock back. Others will never allow me to change. A good-looking woman should not walk down the street naked and a former headhunter should not walk around without guns. I will never walk with my eyes closed through a sea of rattle snakes. No one knows better than me the treacherous nature of the underworld and I will not fall victim to it.

So, while I have given up crime, I have not given up life. Any threat to my life or my loved ones will be seen as a declaration of war.

There will be wiseguys who will want to build a reputation by putting me in my grave. I am hated and bitterly resented. What I have done plays a big part, and the books and the notoriety has added to it. Jealousy is a factor. I would be a retarded fool not to maintain a strong guard.

If you were me what would you do? How would you handle it?

I HAVE a relative who I won't name, because I love him dearly and he is a good old guy. He is a Mason and a member of the RSL. He is a gun collector who believes Australia is being taken over by wogs, greenies, the homosexual lobby and vegetarians. He has gone through roughly 14 television sets in the past 10 years. The evening news and current affairs programmes upset him.

He has this old World War II German Luger 9mm and pulls it out and blasts away at the TV screen.

It is probably just as well that it is just the TV screen and not the real people. He only watches black and white televisions. He, like my father, only watches black and white because he believes colour television puts out infrared rays which send you blind or give you cancer. If he had a colour television then perhaps I could get him a remote control. He could then just turn the bloody thing off or change the channel rather than shooting the box every time. It would save the ammo bill and give the neighbours a break.

I am a picture of mental health compared with some of my relatives that I could name, but won't. Bless their mad hearts.

THE criminal world is populated by three basic types – social spastics, mental retards and brain-dead junkies. There is also a smattering of freaks and flukes.

If you are a social spastic, a mental retard or a brain-dead junkie, or even a freak, and you haven't been caught or jailed, then you are definitely a fluke.

Let me explain a freak to you. A freak in the criminal world is anyone who can lay claim to having half a brain. The rest of the criminal population see such an individual as an intellectual giant possessed with almost God-like intelligence. The rest of the poor slobs, being without the brains of your average dung beetle, see the crook with half a brain as having the IQ of a rocket scientist.

Anyone with a full brain is seen as a freak genius – or a psycho with no ears. Ha ha.

If you don't believe me, spend two weeks in any jail in Australia and you will begin to feel like Albert Einstein.

WHEN a man can admit to himself and others that the world is full of men, twice his size and half his size, who could beat him in a fight, then he is well on the way to never being beaten.

I learned that a long time ago.

Streetfighters are a penny a truckload. Good streetfighters are somewhat harder to find and freak streetfighters are one in a million.

What separates the run of the mill from the freaks is more than a physical thing. It is mind control and thinking ability. Any fool can spend half their life in bars getting into drunken blues with a belly full of Dutch guts. Any drunken mug can whiz out the old Mexican boxing glove and stab an unarmed man in the pub car park.

Any toerag can jump you from behind when your back is turned. But while many will say these tactics are terrible, I am here to tell you they are all legal. Page 267 subsection 7B of the streetfighting section in the robbers' rule book clearly states that any and all means are legal. In streetfighting there are only winners and losers. There are no rules.

In the midst of all this chaos how can you tell the top of the range fighter from the mug? That is easy. The freak streetfighter wins nearly all his fights without throwing a punch.

Death never brawls in the street. Death never has to throw a punch. Death only smiles, puts his hand inside his coat and says in a quiet voice, 'Excuse me, mate, I didn't quite hear that. Were you talking to me?'

Men found blown away in car parks have generally been stupid enough to invite death outside for a fist fight.

Death never has to raise his voice or his fist in anger. The most polite and well-mannered gent you will ever meet in the world is the hangman.

In the world of the streetfighter, the smiling death adder beats the roaring lion every time. As for karate and martial arts experts, a different form of logic is needed to combat them, and this is called Belfast logic. When faced with an enemy waving his black belt in your face, I just like to remind them that I am the holder of the black belt in Irish karate, skilled in the ancient Irish art of letting go with the sawn-off double-barrelled shotgun through the dunny door, then running like hell.

In the end, the secret to everything is to think like a rattlesnake and smile like a used car salesman. And for goodness sake, don't get that piece of advice the wrong way around. Be polite, be friendly, be nonaggressive, see trouble and avoid it, but if trouble forces itself upon you, strike first and strike hard, just like a rattlesnake.

On most occasions, even the dim-witted know when they are in the presence of death. Dave the Jew was on his way to commit a cold-blooded murder, wearing a false beard and a wig. He was dressed like a Rabbi, walking through a street in East St Kilda, carrying a bag which contained a machine pistol, loaded with a 15-shot clip, which fired .22 calibre magnum bullets.

A carload of drunken louts pulled up alongside him and drove along the side of the footpath at the same pace as the Jew was walking. They were yelling abuse and teasing this 'Rabbi'. It was about 8pm and one of the louts opened the back door of the car and was about to get out.

The Jew stopped walking, put his hand into the carry bag and, without producing the weapon, took hold of it and aimed the end of the bag towards the car.

No one would have noticed what the Jew had done. Then he just stood and smiled at the car full of hoods. They looked back. It may have been those big, blue, crazy eyes. It must have been something. The driver of the car said, 'Leave him, let's go.' The Jew was all set to pull the trigger. There was about five louts in the car and for 20 to 30 seconds they were standing on the edge of their graves, and they never even knew it. Or did they? Maybe the driver sensed something.

The man who is the most dangerous is the stone killer, or the snap killer, as the Jew calls them. He is the man prepared to kill at the first sign of danger.

A stone killer gives off a vibe most people can feel. The fool is the man who cannot feel it. The graveyards are full with the rotting bodies of fools who have not picked up the feelings.

But the wise man can pick up the feelings from the stone killer. Maybe the driver of that car was a wise man. There is no doubt his decision to move at that second saved him and his four mates.

In the movies you may see the big guy with all the muscles stand over the smaller one. In real life it is strength of mind rather than size of biceps which decides the pecking order.

The art of the streetfighter is to get in and get out with great haste and no fuss. The best ones never even get a drop of blood on their clothing.

It comes down to attitude and thinking ability. If a man with a weak mind tried to confront a man with a strong mind, the fight would not even start. The weak mind would sense the stronger one and surrender without a fight. The weak-minded individual would behave like a small child in the presence of God.

There are men who are great fighters who will lie down to a stone killer. The fighter may be stronger, better, faster but he lacks the guts and the cold-blooded mentality to confront death. He knows that even if he wins the fight, he will lose in the end if he is not prepared to kill.

The psychology of fear is deeper than many people think.

I HAVE outlined the theory before that lust attacks the groin first, the brain second and then the heart. Love attacks the heart first, the brain second and then the groin. Fear attacks only the brain, then cripples every other part of the body.

Many people can control lust and to some degree control love, but few can control fear once it takes hold. Few men have learned to control fear as few men have to confront real fear in their whole lives. I am not talking about going to the dentist or facing an angry wife with a frying pan. I am talking about facing the circumstances where your life may be on the line, and you know it. How you react and what you do may be the difference between life and death.

Love, lust and hate are the basic emotions and feelings that the average person deals with. Fear is not something the average person has to confront or even wishes to confront in an average lifetime. So using fear and controlling it is not something that the average person has to do.

The basic fear that sits in all men's hearts is that each man knows himself. Despite the opinions of others, every man is aware that deep down he is not as good as others think, and that, one day, that may be exposed.

It may be a moral or a physical thing. The man may be not as moral or as true as others believe and he fears that one day he will be exposed as a pretender. It is the same on the physical side: we know the truth about ourselves and in that knowledge is the seed of fear.

One man threatens to attack another. Abuse from both sides is tossed about freely. Then fear sets in. The man who made the threat fears the other may stand his ground, forcing him to carry out his threat, thus bringing untold trouble down on his head. If the man making the threats is confronted and does not have the courage to kill, then he will look a fool.

The man who has been threatened believes or fears that if he doesn't stand his ground he will be made to look weak in the eyes of others.

Sometimes pride outweighs the desire for self-preservation. In the eyes of many, what other people think of you is more important than anything else. The fear of looking weak and foolish in the eyes of others overshadows the fear of death itself. But the fear of death is still real. So you see, in this sort of confrontation, we have two men very frightened for their own reasons.

But if one man uses fear as an ally, rather than an enemy, he will be the one to come out on top. Fear can be used as a weapon against one's enemies, or you can turn it on yourself. Either way it can decide the battle.

Playing games with the mind of the other, with no real intention of acting in a physical manner, one can control fear. I will give you a basic schoolyard example. When one school kid threatens to tell the mother of another about little Billy's wrong doing, little Billy can be controlled by his own fear of being exposed.

Kill one, scare a thousand, because the next person has to believe that you will kill him. Through that belief you control his actions. Many frightened men protect their inner selves with a loud voice, tough talk and a threatening manner, so as to frighten the world away in a lifelong effort not to be exposed.

A truly violent man may adopt a smiling, kindly warm-hearted manner to put others at ease. Courage has nothing to do with it. Frightened men are dangerous men. Confront a rat in a corner and the rat wants to run away and hide – but when he cannot escape, it is fear, not courage, which drives him to attack. So to put fear in the hearts of others for no logical reason is counterproductive.

This is why the loud-mouthed bully boy is nothing to fear. In fact, all men should try to come to grips with fear. When faced with danger remember that fear is a natural emotion; it is there for a reason. You are not a coward because you feel fear. It is there to stop us tongue-kissing tiger snakes. It has its natural place, but it must never be allowed to cloud the mind. I have seen people crippled with fear for no logical reason. And the person who does not understand his own fear cannot use fear against others.

Fear is a phantom, a puff of smoke that can be blown into the eyes to cloud the mind and thoughts. It can destroy logic and reason if you do not understand it. How true is the saying, 'We have nothing to fear but fear itself'.

Men also use fear as a weapon against women. Fear of rejection, of being left alone, of what others will think, of hurting another, of being found out – the list is endless. The female should understand that some men use fear to keep her in her place – to control her in the hope that mind and heart control will lead to pants control.

Women understand sex, but they do not understand the psychology of fear. For women the answer is simple. Understand what is happening to you and if you don't like it, smile, play along nicely and stab the bastard in the back at the first opportunity. Ha, ha.

IT SEEMS to me that men, in or out of prison, are all very impressed with the martial arts, and eager to tell my good self, and anyone else who will listen, that they have a black belt in this and a black belt in that.

It is my view that the mystic oriental fighting arts are over-rated to the extreme. I think that the film makers of Hollywood and Hong Kong have a lot to answer for. People think if they can learn to spin about like a can can dancer throwing high kicks and squealing in high-pitched voices then they must be fighting machines.

Personally, I think the most lethal thing to come out of Asia is bad dim sims. If all the martial arts were the winning weapons their fans claim, why don't we see those well-known pacifists, the IRA, running around the streets of Belfast kicking British soldiers under their double chins?

While I have met some worthwhile fellows who can fight like thrashing machines and are karate experts, it is interesting to note that they could all fight well long before they ever took up martial arts.

It is pretty simple really. If you can't hold your hands up, can't fight or haven't got the stomach for real blood and guts combat, then a black, purple or pink belt is not going to help you much. Good fighters love the battle. A million karate lessons, or boxing lessons, for that matter, will not make a coward a brave man.

Some people who learn karate do it because, deep down, they are the worst combination, cowards with a violent streak. No matter how good they get, they will always back down against a man they fear may be their equal. They just use their fistic skills to frighten and beat up people physically inferior to themselves.

Funny, isn't it, but I never seem to have that much trouble with those sorts of characters.

When I have been asked if I am a karate expert, I have to explain that I am the proud holder of the Irish black belt, the most feared martial arts known to man.

It works every time.

IT HAS reached what used to be my ears that certain members of the criminal world with literary delusions have stated, via their publicist, that they wish to share their profits with victims of crime and worthy charities. At hearing this, my heart strings went twang and I was quite touched. To think that these drag queens have been standing in the shadows of fantasy for so long, they can no longer see the daylight of reality. These so-called big name crooks are, in reality, petty little nobodies who have been swept under the rug of criminal history. So, for fear they will not be remembered for being anything but the insignificant bugs they really are, they employ publicists to promote their causes.

I know that I am a bit of a cynic, so I thought about it for a while, and I have seen the light. If I have any money left after I have paid my legal bill, I too will join the world of the crims turned charity workers. I will open the 'Hole In The Head Home For Old Ratbags'.

I can see it now ... The Mad Dog kitchen, with curries a specialty. And the Beach Ball-Frankie Waghorn dining room, where if you didn't finish your meal you'd get a punch in the mouth. We could have the Alex Tsakmakis gymnasium and weight-lifting room, but watch out you don't crack your head on the weights like old Alex did. There would also be the Craig Minogue weight loss and slimming centre. After that you could go to the Cowboy Johnny Harris Memorial Swimming Pool for a dip.

For the retired crim who wanted to study law, we would have the Anita Betts Legal Library available to 21 members. You could swing a few clubs at the Billy Longley golf course and the bedrooms would be in the Horatio Morris Wing, bringing a new meaning to 'lights out'.

Anyone with a mental problem could go to the Keithy Faure

Group Therapy Room, so you could sit around telling each other lies. We would also have the Ted Eastwood music room. Any complaints would be dealt with in the Dave the Jew room, after which you would never be seen again, unless it was to appear via the Mad Dog's kitchen in the form of a nice curry.

All cash and valuables could be kept in the Christopher Skase room and if you wanted a beer it could be ordered at the Pat Shannon Bar.

The truth is that I will never make enough money to buy anything for anybody. I have a team of lawyers to support. After all, charity begins at home.

CHAPTER 12

JACKALS AND HYENAS

'... HE WOULD LOAD UP A LIGHT AIRCRAFT
WITH EXPLOSIVES AND FLY INTO THE
POLICE ACADEMY, KAMIKAZE STYLE'

In March 1986, Constable Angela Taylor was killed when a stolen car packed with gelignite exploded outside Melbourne's Russell Street police station. It was an act which shocked Australia. An elite police taskforce was set up to catch the gang responsible. Police arrested six men. Two were convicted. Craig Minogue was found guilty of Taylor's murder and sentenced to 28 years, and career criminal Stan Taylor got life.

PAUL Kurt Hetzel was once a member of the most dangerous group in any prison in Australia. He was a member of the Overcoat Gang, the group of men who were led by me in a five-year war inside Pentridge which resulted in at least 100 bashings and 11 attempted murders over five years.

Each member of the gang was crazy, tough and gutsy. All except Hetzel, who was eventually kicked out of the gang on the grounds of cowardice in the face of the enemy. He was flung on orders from me and Jimmy Loughnan, my one-time mate who ended up turning on me.

Hetzel was one of the most evil men I have ever met, and I have not exactly lived a sheltered life when it comes to matters involving bad men. He was treacherous, cunning, cruel and the master manipulator, with a psychopathic hatred of police. He had once gunned down a copper during an armed robbery. Hetzel and Stan Taylor had been an old partnership for many years, in and out of jail. When Hetzel was a member of the Overcoat Gang in H Division in 1976–77, he often raved on about his dreams of killing police.

Hetzel once told me that if he ever found out that he was dying of cancer, or any other fatal disease, he would load up a light aircraft with explosives and fly into the Police Academy, Kamikaze style. He would talk at length about his dreams of murdering police and always had explosives as the preferred method of killing as many as possible.

Jimmy Loughnan and myself were used to big-noting nitwits who raved on about what they wanted to do. We dismissed Hetzel as a dreamer, but a dangerous one. His mate, Stan Taylor, was also a great one for voicing his dreams of ambushing police in some fantasy death trap. But it was Hetzel who always struck me as a man possessed with this line of thought.

Craig 'Slim' Minogue actually called me as a defence witness in the Russell Street bombing trial, to give evidence against Hetzel, who was the star witness for the Crown. He was probably the heaviest protected police witness in Australian history.

The idea of calling Chopper Read to discredit a star witness was not considered a good idea. It was even suggested by the prosecution that the real reason for calling me was for me to say something stupid and have the trial aborted so Slim could get another trial.

All I would have said is what I knew about Hetzel. But a man with no ears and a reputation like mine would not have done Minogue much good. In fact, the jury probably would have questioned the sanity of someone like Craig simply because he knew me.

The fact still remains that one of the masters of madness, Paul K.

Hetzel, who put together the blueprint, strategy and tactics of the Russell Street bombing, went on to be a witness for the Crown.

He ended up being protected by the police that he hated so much. The mastermind escaped, leaving the workers to cop the rap. I often wonder what the police really thought of that arrangement and what result they ended up with. Two convicted out of six ... Stan 'King of the Kids' Taylor, the so-called boss of the gang, and Craig 'Slim' Minogue, whose role in the whole affair was that of odd job boy. He was kept in the dark most of the time.

Craig's role in this huge crime wave was to spend most of his time lounging back in a large Jason Rocker recliner, with a telephone in one hand and a family-size pizza, with extra cheese and mushrooms, in the other.

Slim Minogue had top connections in the automotive industry. The whole crew was supposed to be a car theft gang. They were supposed to knock off top-of-the-range cars, motorbikes, caravans and boats. They would have made big bucks.

The bomb idea was the brain child of Taylor and Hetzel. Minogue launched into the thing after the event in the name of friendship and loyalty. He wanted to protect his friends and his baby brother. I believe he was guilty, but not as guilty as some others and certainly not as guilty as many people think.

I believe Minogue became involved after the event, embarking on a form of damage control which was doomed from the start. Taylor and Hetzel kept him in the dark before the event because they were both terrified of him. He was the sleeping bear of the gang and when he did wake up, it was too late.

Minogue once told me that if the young policewoman, Angela Taylor, had not been killed in the bombing, and if no one had been killed, then the investigation may have been conducted in a different way with more thought and less emotion.

Minogue was living high on the hog, with no shortage of money, power or luxury. He was the physical power behind the whole crew. He was an honest crook. Evil treachery was not part of his make-up. In the end, he found himself with two masters of double dealing in Hetzel and Taylor.

Slim simply sank in a sea of treachery, while the rest of the crew scrambled for the boats. He kept his mouth shut as he sank, with more knives in his back than Julius Caesar.

Hetzel played them all like a violin. I believe he beat the cops, his old gang and the courts. To catch a fox, the police ended up kissing a rattlesnake. The rest of the gang, including Slim, were only bunnies in Hetzel's treacherous game.

TERRORISM, whether it be political or criminal, rarely achieves what people hope it will. It normally is a massive failure. The IRA has been blasting the hell out of the British for years and all it has achieved is to make the Brits more determined to dig in. The same with the PLO with the Israelis. The harder one side pushes the more the other one digs in.

In Australia, we have had the Hilton and Russell Street bombings and the shooting of two policemen in Walsh Street. All three acts can be classed as terrorism and what did they achieve? They only strengthened the resolve of the politicians, police and the public. The immediate response is to give the police more funds and power. It strengthens the resolve of the police and bonds them together. If anything, it makes the police a tougher enemy.

It seems to me that terrorism is a weapon of anger and not of intelligence.

The use of terror tactics by criminals against criminals works a treat. It is an underground war where people like me can succeed. But using terror against the people, or the police protecting the people, political targets or any of the armed services, simply won't work.

The only time terrorism works is when the target has no moral outrage. The Jews used terror to kick the Brits out of Palestine, but the Brits needed Palestine like a hole in the head. Terrorism may work against an enemy who believes he is in the wrong, but it will never work against an enemy who believes he is in the right.

Righteous indignation takes over and no force on earth can defeat that.

Terrorism defeats itself when it creates outrage in its victims.

Pavel Vasilof Marinof, a former Bulgarian army deserter turned burglar, was one of the first men to force the Victorian Police to realise that armed conflict in the streets was a reality in Australia.

Marinof, also known as Max Clarke and 'Mad Max', was stopped for questioning by two uniformed police on 19 June. He got out of his car firing and shot both police, leaving one a paraplegic. Two more police were shot as they tried to find the gunman, who was a crack shot.

More than 200 armed police were thrown into the area around Noble Park but the man managed to escape.

The hunt for Mad Max ended eight months later when he was killed in a gunfight with police who pulled over a van he was driving on the Hume Highway at Kal Kallo, north of Melbourne. Desperate to the last, Marinof shot two detectives before he was fatally shot by one of the injured men.

IT is my own personal opinion that the Victoria Police is the most blood-soaked body of men and women in Australian law enforcement history.

They have been baptised in a sea of their own blood, along with the blood and guts of those who went up against them.

It would be hard to pick out the worst and maddest of all these. It is like asking what hurts worse, a .38 calibre slug or a .45 calibre slug in the brain. How do you compare one funeral with another, one act of insanity with another?

When I attacked His Honour, Judge William Martin, in the County Court on 26 January 1978, police said to me that I had just opened a new door and that every nutter in town would upgrade their insanity to match it.

When Amos 'The Witch Doctor' Atkinson took 30 hostages and staged a siege in the Italian Waiters' Club to demand my release from prison, again in 1978, it was the first time the newly-formed Special Operations Group was called out.

My stupid attack on Judge Martin was used by the men in power as the reason to set up the SOG in the first place. When Atkinson pulled the Waiters' Club stunt it confirmed the fact that the SOG did have a role to play.

But how tame that all seems now compared with Walsh Street, Hoddle Street and Queen Street. But an event a few years before that woke the police up to the modern world.

A man no one had heard of walked up and invited the Victoria Police into the cold world of modern day reality.

The police force changed overnight because of one man. It wasn't the Commissioner or the Police Minister, it was some crazy Bulgarian named Mad Max, Pavel Marinof. Compared with Mad Max, the rest of the nutters wouldn't last three rounds with a revolving door.

I have always believed that your greatest enemies are your best teachers and this is true for everyone, including police.

Every time they go to a funeral or get blood splashed in their eyes, they learn and come out of it stronger, and, in my opinion, Mad Max taught the police more in 60 seconds than they had learned in the previous 60 years.

We go to the movies or watch television and marvel at the lunatics in America. But I have no doubt that pound for pound the Australian-grown nutter is madder than anything the Yanks have to offer.

The only difference is that, in America, they make a movie about their crazies five minutes after they are arrested or killed. In Australia, we tend to forget about them and tell ourselves that it could only happen in America.

The police learned from Mad Max. They learned that no matter how tough you are, how hard you are, how much you think you know, there is always some whacked-out, head-banging lunatic waiting around the corner ready and willing to teach you a little bit more.

Mad Max, for one reason or another, was a lesson to us all.

CHAPTER 13

SHANNON GOT DEAD, THE TEXAN GOT LIFE

'ON THE NIGHT OF SHANNON'S DEATH …
HIS MINDERS SEEMED NOT AS ALERT AS THEY
SHOULD HAVE BEEN. MANY PEOPLE KNEW
IT WAS COMING, BUT THEY DIDN'T BOTHER
TO WARN PAT'

In the 1970s, while in jail in Melbourne, Read stuck his nose into an underworld war which had little to do with him. The Painters and Dockers Union was made up of hard men and violent criminals. A particularly vicious election battle for the control of the union ended with the union secretary, Pat Shannon, being shot dead in the bar of the Druids Hotel in South Melbourne on 17 October 1973.

A well-known docker and former member of the union executive, Billy 'the Texan' Longley, was charged with the murder. The Crown claimed Longley had paid another man, Kevin Taylor, $6,000 to have the job done.

Longley served 13 years over the murder, but always claimed he was innocent. Years later, he spoke out to The Bulletin *magazine detailing allegations of crime and corruption involving the union. This resulted in the Costigan Royal Commission into the Painters and Dockers.*

Longley's decision to break his silence did not help his popularity in some circles. Read liked Longley and, never frightened of unpopularity, vowed to protect 'the Texan' while they were both inside. The pair eventually walked out of jail intact. But many of their enemies did not.

THE beauty of being in jail is that everyone knows where you are and they can drop you a line when they feel like it. And, of course, I have plenty of time to deal with all sorts of serious correspondence.

I have received heaps of mail from people who have read *Chopper One* and *Two*, and some feel that I seem to have some sort of hang-up about the Victorian Federated Ship Painters and Dockers Union. Some people who wrote to me were old dockies themselves, many of whom I personally like. Others were brain-dead blockheads who must have got their parole officers to scratch their thoughts out in crayon.

But I think it is fair that I explain my relationship with some of the members of the union, which has had control of many elements of the Victorian crime world.

Let me make it clear, my friendship and loyalty to Billy Longley goes a long way back. I didn't decide to shed blood and protect him from half the knife-wielding population of Pentridge because I was bored. It wasn't a case of saying: 'Hey, there's nothing on TV, let's start a prison war which will go on for years.' Despite popular opinion to the contrary, I'm just not that crazed.

In my first book, I stated I had first met Billy in the can in 1976. Well let me confess, dear reader, the old Chop Chop told a little prudent white lie there. Let me put it this way, at the time of writing *Chopper*, I was in jail awaiting parole and I felt, along with my handpicked team of drunken advisers, that it was legally unwise to reveal certain matters which may or may not have happened involving The Texan and my good self, prior to 1976.

After all, it was basically ancient history, and my bloody business at any rate.

Let me simply say that perhaps I knew a little bit more about the Painters and Dockers War of the 1970s than what I read in the newspapers. I have sailed very close to the legal wind on some of the things I have written, and I have no intention of sailing into a legal hurricane over stuff that happened 20 years ago.

I have shown myself particularly stupid over the years but even I baulk at the concept of total legal suicide.

Let me tell you a few details about the untimely death of poor Pat Shannon. Senior members of the union, Mr Louey Wright, Jack 'Putty Nose' Nicholls and Bobby 'Machine Gun' Dix, all had one thing in common ... they wanted to see both Shannon and Billy Longley out of the way.

Old Louey Wright was a waterfront power broker, controlling things from behind the scenes while keeping a low profile. He was collecting 10 ghost pay packets a week for his own pocket, and that was seen as only a petty perk for the man.

It was Louey Wright who controlled the crew who controlled Pat Shannon. Shannon has been painted as a mastermind, but the truth is he was only the front man for others. Sometimes front men can be exactly that and other times they start to believe their own publicity. Old Louey ended up with a little problem. Pat started to believe what people were saying about him and thought he was some sort of waterfront politician. He was getting a wee bit too big for his boots and started to forget who put him where he was. He was a puppet, not a boss, but he began to see himself in a different light.

Pat Shannon was a popular man and he was gaining his own power base on the docks. Many of the workers started to believe in him. But these admirers did not include Louey Wright and company. Machine Gun Bobby was a Shannon man, but he was not so blind as to ignore the real waterfront Godfather, old Louey. So Bobby gave his loyalty to two masters, both Shannon and Wright. Shannon had powerful friends in the political area. He had friends in the Labour Party, amongst some police, in legal circles and with the underworld. He had the full support of some heavy crooks including the Kane brothers, Jackie Twist and several other strong men. He was on the way up and nothing but a bullet with his name on it was going to stop him.

Pat Shannon's contact list included men from the ACTU, several union leaders, newspaper and television journalists. He was a mover and shaker, but he was also greedy, a fatal flaw. Then along came Billy Longley, a popular, powerful and feared waterfront personality, who tossed his hat into the election ring on an anti-commie ticket. 'Let's get these bloody commies off the docks,' Billy used to yell.

Shannon had some powerful friends in other unions who were communists. This meant that every commie on the waterfront backed Shannon against Longley. Shannon was recruiting even more powerful backers. Sometimes Dockie politics gets a little bit exciting, and on this occasion a real shooting war broke out. Meanwhile old Louey Wright watched and waited. Anger and hate towards Billy Longley drove Putty Nose Nicholls and Bobby Dix further into the Shannon camp.

Old Louey was forgotten in all the blood, chaos and bullets that was the election campaign. It was a bad mistake. I don't care how hot things were getting, you should never leave someone like old Louey out of business calculations.

Three weeks before the Shannon shooting, Jackie Twist met Louey in a Port Melbourne hotel. It was a private conversation. Twist left the meeting to visit various men close to Shannon. Twist passed on a clear message: 'This shit must stop'.

Now Twist was not a man to be argued with. He was the one who croaked Freddie 'The Frog' Harrison with a shotgun in broad daylight on the docks in the 1950s and he was a feared and respected figure.

He told them all that the war must end and that both Shannon and Longley must go.

Many of the men in the Shannon camp knew that Pat was off tap, that he was to die. It came as no surprise when he got his. Longley was supposed to die on the same night. And at least two others, a Shannon strong man and another major waterfront figure, were also supposed to go on the missing list.

Shannon expressed his fears about Louey Wright to Alfred 'The Ferret' Nelson. The Ferret was later to scream his lungs out and tell all before his very painful death as part of the war. His body was never found and, let me assure you, it never will be.

Shannon tried to get Brian Kane to kill Louey Wright, but Louey and Brian's father, Reggie, were very close, which was very unfortunate for Shannon.

On the night of Shannon's death he was caught off-guard and his minders seemed not as alert as they should have been. At least one key Shannon man was nowhere to be seen at the time of the killing. He must have just stepped out for a minute. Many people knew it was coming, but they didn't bother to warn Pat. Kevin Taylor was supposed to be working for Billy Longley, but was he really? I have always had severe doubts on that count.

Taylor claimed he did the hit for five grand on the nod, on credit. Now I have heard many strange things, but I don't know of any sensible gunman who would agree to a shoot now, pay later credit plan. Taylor claimed he was put up to it by Longley and that he never even got paid for it. I would have given him 20 years for stupidity if that was the case.

Taylor screamed Longley's name long and loud when he was arrested and questioned. Taylor later told me he only gave Longley up because he believed Billy was dead. If Taylor believed that the Texan was on the missing list, he must have had intimate knowledge of the plans of others.

Taylor was a small part of a bigger plan. Whether the Texan had Shannon whacked or not is beside the point. Longley was the victim of a treacherous waterfront chess game put together by some of Shannon's so-called mates. They cheated Longley out of his lawful election victory, then set Shannon up for a bullet, and Longley for a life sentence. I know that Billy the Texan hated Shannon's guts and badly wanted to see him dead. But I don't believe for a moment that Longley hired a nitwit like Kevin Bloody Taylor to do it.

Longley could have called on any number of top people from Ray Chuck to Jimmy the Pom to Vincent Villeroy. I would have been happy to do it if I had been asked, so why Kevin Taylor? Old Louey Wright, Jackie Twist and Bobby Dix took a lot of secrets to the grave, including the real truth about the Shannon killing.

If Billy was behind the Shannon killing, he couldn't have pulled it off without the help of some of Shannon's men. Longley got set up and given up. It is all over now, but nothing is ever forgotten or forgiven. Just ask Kevin Taylor. Oh, I forgot, you can't. He got his right whack in Pentridge.

Longley and Shannon hated each other but they had one thing in common: they wanted to change the face of the waterfront. After the war, after people went on the missing list, after the funerals and after the trials, Shannon and Longley were gone from the union. Then the old established power brokers surfaced and things went back to normal. They were the only ones who would win from having both men out of the way. They placed all the blame on the Texan to wash away their own sins.

CHAPTER 14

THE THOUGHTS OF CHAIRMAN MARK

'THE PENTRIDGE HEAD SHRINK ONCE
SAID TO ONE, "CHOPPER, YOU'RE NOT MAD.
YOU'RE JUST A BAD BASTARD."'

SID Collins has done for the Outlaws motorcycle club what Jack the Ripper did for women's liberation. As a force in the 'one per cent' motorcycle world they are now viewed with suspicion. If their former president turned out to be a nark and a police informer and Crown witness then how does that help the so-called solid-as-a-rock reputation of the Outlaws motorcycle club in general?

Some comedian sent a telegram to the Outlaws' Launceston headquarters, at 42 Mayne Street in Invermay, requesting that the club not make any phone calls during Operation NOAH. Ha ha. Another joke in the bike world is that when the Outlaws say they are 'one percenters' it means there is a 99 per cent chance they will spill their guts in a police station. I will, however, say that there are some rock-solid good blokes in the club, and Sid Collins' sins should not be held against all of them. But I will also say that not one member of the Outlaws lifted a finger to try to stop Sid giving evidence against me. Forgive me for being unkind, but I was sent to prison – for life, maybe – on the false evidence of a former president of the Outlaws.

Since being in Risdon I have received a lovely letter from Craig

'Slim' Minogue sending me regards and hellos from an old mate of mine and former Overcoat Gang member 'Bluey B'. They are in the same yard and Slim was telling me that he found out recently that three Crown witnesses in his case, who for some reason were not given police protection, spent two years hiding out under the protection of the Vigilante motorcycle club – one of these witnesses having friends in that area. Slim says that the moral and conduct code of a lot of these so-called rough bike gangs is highly suspect. The only club in that scene whose reputation cannot be called into question is the Hell's Angels.

I am very bitter inside about this Collins bullshit. While I put on a happy face and maintain my normal smiling self I am not happy inside. It is something I will not forget. Collins, and any friend and supporter of Collins, would be well advised to avoid me in future. Trent Anthony and his friends would be wise to do the same. There are other so-called friends in Launceston who did not put out the hand of friendship towards me in my time of need. These human scum, who I will not name, will not be forgotten either.

And I am a man with a long, long memory. Shallow people and false pretenders don't have long memories. They will forget, but I won't. I don't have to shoot people to punish them. There are more ways to kill a cat than by wringing its neck. The cats in question used up their nine lives when they betrayed my trust and friendship, let me tell you.

As I have stated before, to me revenge is a holy duty. It is not something to be loudmouthed about in pubs, or to bignote about. It is not just something that 'should be done', but something that 'must be done'. In some way, either by my own hand or by my hand guiding the hand of another, I have always had my revenge. In the revenge department I see myself as something of a puppet master. I didn't kill Alex Tsakmakis, but he is dead. Billy 'the Texan' Longley didn't personally kill 'Putty Nose' Nicholls but Putty Nose is dead. I didn't kill Shane Goodfellow, but he is dead. I didn't kill Paul Brough or Big Dave Dominguez, but they are dead. It's all chess. It's just the way you place your pawns, your rooks, your knights and your bishops. It's all a game and it's a game I'm good at. As I've said before, revenge is a dish best eaten cold, and time is my friend, not my enemy.

I'VE HAD a lot of time to think about things lately, and I remembered something from when I was a kid. When I was about 10 or 11 years of age there was this wrecker's yard in the area where we lived, full of junk cars and trucks. This yard was protected by a high chain wire fence topped with barbed wire and four guard dogs.

Three of the dogs were all bark and no bite, but the fourth was the meanest junkyard dog God ever shovelled guts into. It was a large, mongrel-bred, crazy-eyed killer which seemed in a non-stop frenzy. The other kids used to feed and pat the good dogs through the fence and tease and torment the savage dog, tossing rocks at it and delighting at its rage. But none of the kids could get into the wrecker's yard. I, on the other hand, would go down to the yard alone and befriend the mad dog and offer him my lunch. And over a period of time I could even pat him through the fence. He was a dirty, ugly, evil beast but he ended up trusting me and would greet me with tail wagging and eat the food I offered. One day I climbed the fence. I was the only kid the crazy dog would allow into the yard. That was my first practical lesson in tactical psychology and I have studied it ever since. That and what I call 'human chess' has helped me stay alive in the face of overwhelming odds.

But it stands to reason that no man can win every battle, argument or chess game. Napoleon was a tactical combat genius, whereas Wellington was a la-de-dah tea-drinking powder puff with limited experience ... but look what happened.

Sid Collins and Trent Anthony did to me what I did to that guard dog all those years ago, and I couldn't see it happening.

THERE is a young Englishman in Risdon Prison called 'Pommy Mick' who knows Sid Collins. Around September 1991, according to Pommy Mick, Collins was involved in a questionable deal. A punch-on broke out between the two men in the car park of the Mowbray Hotel in Launceston. Collins ran off and fired two shots at Mick with a small calibre handgun. Two weeks later, Pommy Mick ambushed Collins as he came out of the Park Hotel and fired shots at him. Neither men could hit the side of a barn. Not a drop of blood hit the footpath in either case.

Mick was going to make a second attempt on Collins and his friend and sometimes bodyguard Black Uhlans Larry around December that year – but was told Collins was a friend of mine, as it was that month that I first met Collins. I had always been told that Collins had only befriended me for reasons of his own personal safety. Pommy Mick was only one of those reasons. This Mick might not be able to shoot straight but he is a cold-blooded young madman who hopes to meet Mr Collins again one day, which would be very pleasant as far as I'm concerned.

It appears there is a rather long list of men who are looking to kill Collins and his offsider Larry, so they needed someone like me as protection. And I'm supposed to be the tactician. I'm ashamed. In matters of tactical warfare and violence I am the best, but Margaret always said I was too soft-hearted and trusting with people I felt were my friends. And Margaret, as always, was right.

SPEAKING of Sid Collins, if Sid believes in omens he'd better start worrying about his will and what sort of flowers he wants on his grave, because I had an insane dream recently that I was at his funeral.

In the dream, Renee Brack, the 'Hard Copy' television reporter, was conducting the service and my old mates Dave the Jew and Horatio Morris were the gravediggers. I was chief mourner – and then Sid appeared and stood beside me and told me he was sorry and asked me to forgive him. He told me he had hired Anita Betts, as he was going to sue the president of the Hell's Angels for killing him. And he told me his mate had run off with his wife Simone.

I did exactly what I'd like to do in real life: pulled out a gun and shot Sid in the head. Then Trent Anthony jumped out of the crowd yelling, 'I saw that! I saw that!' Anita Betts then attacked Trent Anthony – so Sid yelled out to her that she was fired. Then Damien Bugg (the prosecutor who got me put away) rushed in and tried to bandage Sid's half-blown-away head. Anita turned around and yelled out, 'Who invited that bastard?'

I turned to see Mr Justice Cox (the trial judge in the Collins case) and I said: 'I hope you're taking note of all this' and he replied that he wasn't allowed to talk to me. So I shot him in the head. Trent Anthony broke free from Anita and screamed, 'I saw that!' Then I shot Trent in the head, and it was Sid's turn to yell out, 'I saw that.' Billy 'the Texan' Longley appeared. I said, 'What are you doing here?' He said he was visiting Pat Shannon's grave. Damien Bugg then tried to arrest Billy the Texan. Meanwhile, Renee Brack was telling her offsider to get it all on film. I began to walk away from this graveside chaos – and Ita Buttrose marched past me, really angry. I said, 'What's wrong, Ita?' and she said, 'That bloody Renee Brack has just pinched my camera.'

It was all too much for me. Bloody hell, I was relieved when I woke up. But I have to say that when I dream I have vivid dreams in full living colour, as if it is all real. Doctors have told me that my ultra-vivid dreams have nothing to do with any psychiatric disorder, but maybe they're just being nice to the man with no ears. Let me tell you that I have some 1,000 per cent LSD acid trips when I dream. I'm a solid sleeper as a rule and don't dream much, but when I do it's worth the wait. They seem to go on all night and have a cast of thousands. I can meet someone once and two days later the bugger can jump into my dream.

I often dream that I'm caught in a life and death situation and I reach for my gun and it isn't there. Or I get stuck in a chess game that won't end. Once, three nights in a row, I dreamed I mowed the lawn over and over again and never seemed to finish it. I often die in my dreams and go to either heaven or hell. When I fall from tall buildings I always seem to land.

I've got a mad sense of humour and a lot of my dreams are very comical, at least to my good self. During the Collins trial, I was dreaming nearly every night and in one of them Sammy the Turk (Siam Ozerkam, shot dead by Read in June 1987) gave evidence against me, saying that I shot him in the eye. And Anita Betts asked him, 'Where did this happen?' and he said in the back of Sid's car. Then the barrister Boris Kayser swept into the court room and yelled, 'Your Honour, this man is dead. Will the Crown stop at nothing?'

The judge was none other than my old mate Vincent Villeroy, and he agreed with Mr Kayser and ordered Sammy the Turk reburied. Damien Bugg was no longer prosecuting. He had become foreman of the jury, and Trent Anthony was on the jury and so was my mother and my sister, and Craig Minogue (convicted of the Russell Street bombing) was the prosecutor. My dear old dad was sitting in the public gallery in full Masonic regalia holding his Enfield .303 rifle. Sid Collins was sitting beside me in the dock, and Frankie Waghorn was assisting Anita Betts with the defence.

The screw sitting in the dock with us was one I'd known at H Division, wearing full Ku Klux Klan robes and hood. Collins was shitting himself. There was a massive argument raging between Anita Betts and Craig Minogue. Slim was arguing that Julian Knight shot Sid as he was driving down Hoddle Street. Anita Betts then accused my old mate Micky Marlow of doing it. Micky stood up and said, 'No, no. Tony Tanner did it.' Vincent Villeroy then asked me if Sid Collins was a member of the Victorian Federated Painters and Dockers. The screw in the KKK robes started to kick Sid Collins in

the head, and Boris Kayser yelled out, 'Your Honor!' The dream
went on like this all night: total chaos, with everyone from Margaret
to Cowboy Johnny Harris and Tracy Warren yelling abuse from the
public gallery while I sat in the dock.

The dream ended with Vincent Villeroy pulling out a firearm
from behind the bench and shooting every member of the jury, while
Sid and I returned to the cells with Anita telling Sid that if he told the
truth she would get him off with a fine.

And the psychiatrists reckon there's nothing wrong with me. Ha
ha ha.

WHEN I came to Tassie in November 1991, I had already arranged,
or should I say, it had been agreed between my good self and some
other gentlemen (who could be said to be enemies of mine) that I be
paid a small but regular sling sent to me care of a post box number. I
saw it as my 'stay away money'. It was only a grand a month from
men who spent a grand a night on dinner and drinks and girls, so it
was only petty cash to them. But it was the principle that was
important. I am a man of principle, especially when it comes to
money. Why shouldn't I collect a sling, after all? I was going to
Tassie, which meant their wish had come true. I wasn't planning on
returning, which they thought was wonderful. Technically, I had
won the war, so why should I walk away with nothing? But a grand
a month soon gets spent on the basics of life and the money ran out
quickly every month. The deal had been struck while I was in jail,
and a grand a month seemed good at that time. It lasted right up to
my coming to Risdon jail but won't be continuing – unless, of course,
I return to Melbourne to renegotiate, which I won't be doing in the
near future. The criminal culture of Melbourne sees the sling as an
acceptable part of doing business. The parties concerned wanted
peace, so it seemed only fair that I get a small piece of the action. The
size of the sling is not the issue. It is a simple matter of personal

respect – of 'face', as the Japs like to call it. If anybody had found out about it, the other side would have lost face, so I said nothing. But my little sling is now over, so what's the harm?

Because I went back to jail for the Sid Collins incident, the total sling ended up being only $7,000 altogether. Big deal. I could have snipped them for a much bigger sling, but that would have meant them trying to kill me … and me having to retaliate. The grand in the hand every month was a token offering that pleased both sides. So to them who thought I left Melbourne because of the fearsome might of my enemies, think again. I wanted to leave, and I'd had enough, and I was being paid. So don't believe all the shit you hear in nightclubs.

OVER the years, I have had various hush hush police from the federal internal investigations department, the Victoria Police IID and internal security unit come to see me over various matters. One funny memory was when a member of the Victoria Police ISU was flicking through the pages of my address book, which he had seized to find his own name, rank squad, address and phone number listed. Ha, ha. I collect details of various police like a punter collects details on racehorses, even down to car registration numbers. Why? Because it could be useful one day. Apart from anything else, I love to see their faces when they find out I know at least as much about them as they do about me.

I have always found these secret hush hush police from the various internal investigation units given to unhealthy paranoia and suspicion, and they all seem to believe in conspiracy theories. This is a wonderful weapon to use against the police themselves, as they are believers in the unbelievable.

The National Crime Authority boys were among the most highly strung group of ultra-paranoid police I've ever dealt with. You could wind them up like robot puppets. They were so paranoid they would speak in whispers while checking the ceiling, walls, floor, table and chairs for hidden listening devices. What a comedy.

I have written before about a federal policeman turned NCA cop called Cedric Netto. He is a serious, no-nonsense honest cop given to just a touch of classic NCA paranoia. Now he is back in the feds and would be one of the most cunning and dangerously honest bastards I've seen in the job. He is a classic example of the mentality and thinking pattern of the people in the internal investigating units within the various police forces, state and federal. Which means I shouldn't have been surprised when, one day in November 1992, the Governor of Risdon called me to his office and asked if I would be willing to talk to a federal policeman who wanted to interview me about my 'involvement and relationship with Cedric Netto'.

'What involvement?' I asked. 'Who is this bloke?' I was told he was from the federal police's internal investigations. What a bloody joke. The poor bloody Launceston CIB found the name 'Cedric Netto' and a phone number (clearly marked 'federal police'!) in my address book, and jumped to the conclusion that Netto was on Captain Chopper's pay roll.

The fact is I've seen Netto about half a dozen times in my life. He has questioned me about various matters, but mostly relating to the late private investigator Tom 'Hopa-long' Ericksen. Netto came out to Pentridge a few times because my name had been tossed up in the ruck in matters he was investigating. As I've said before, he would be the most painfully honest bastard I'd ever met from the federal police or any other police force.

The fact is that whenever I have spoken to Netto I have always been left wondering what it was all about. NCA police leave you thinking, What the hell was that all about?, as they tend not to come to any direct point, but verbally dance around a conversation while looking at the roof and walls for concealed devices, of course. Ha ha. I guess it's a case of if you know Chopper Read you must either be totally corrupt or crazy. Well, Netto is not corrupt. And I am no bloody psychiatrist, so I can't give any sort of opinion as to his mental health.

I had the names of roughly 25 Victorian, Tasmanian and federal police in my address book, also roughly 80 rego numbers taken from unmarked police cars. But Netto's name was the only one clearly marked 'federal police', hence the big investigation. I'd find it comical, except for the fact these internal police investigators have no sense of humour.

THE psychiatrist and psychologist are God's gift to the mentally ill, proving that God does have a sense of humour. Yet again I have been interviewed by yet another psychiatrist, who is quite a nice fellow in himself, not at all like some of the other head-banging, barking mental cases I have seen masquerading as doctors. The psychologist here is a horny-looking honey who obviously can't read minds, because if she could she would put her hands over her arse and run screaming from her office. And the other psychiatrist is a rather friendly fellow and not a bad chap. I was quite taken aback to meet three normal members of the psychiatric profession – psychiatrists being the natural enemy of the psychopath.

Dr Alan Bartholomew, the Pentridge head shrink, once said to me, 'Chopper, you're not mad. You're just a bad bastard'. So much for medical opinion. What more can I say?

OVER the years my never-ending dramas and adventures have taken their toll on my old dad's mental wellbeing and he is no longer the same man he once was. He was always a touch on the aggro and paranoid side, but his paranoia has reached the stage where the old bloke has now totally lost the plot.

During my second trial he wrote to me telling me he had a strong suspicion that Trent Anthony could be a police spy. Considering that

Trent was going Crown witness against me one would hardly need to be a rocket scientist to have a faint sneaking suspicion about him. But when Dad wrote to me telling me he believed my legal problems were a 'Catholic conspiracy' against me I knew that he had well and truly lost track, bless his heart. And when he heard that our old mate Billy 'the Texan' Longley was taking Margaret ballroom dancing he wrote to me wondering if Billy was trying to back door me.

He's a great one for writing letters, is Dad. He wrote to the 'Grand Inspector General of the Supreme Council of the Masonic Lodge' at 10 Duke Street, St James, London, and alerted them to the plight – ha ha, oh my good God – of my good self. Then he contacted the tax department demanding they investigate the financial affairs of not only Trent Anthony and Sid Collins, but the police who arrested me.

Naturally Dad also whizzed off a quick letter to Bruce Ruxton, the Prime Minister and the Tasmanian Premier. He is in constant touch with a crew of World War II army veterans, Masonic Lodge, Orange Lodge and a regular crew of old Right-wing nutters. They also whizz off stern letters to God only knows who re the sorry plight of my good self. Dad feels that Sid Collins could have been involved in drugs, so a stiff letter to the NCA, DEA and American FBI was sent post haste.

He once wrote a letter to the health department because he thought the police station smelled. But I love my old dad. He means well. He sits in his home unit with his guns and thinks about my situation and all the people out to get me, and it sends him around the twist. To him, his son is always in the right.

I've gone up to my dad years ago and said, 'Dad, I had to shoot some bastard tonight.' He'd say, 'Who was that, son?' and I'd say, 'Some wog.' He'd say, 'Ahh, he'd be a bloody catholic. Was he a drug dealer?' I'd say, 'Yes' and he'd ask, 'Did you put one in the head, son?' If I said no, he'd say, 'You should have killed the bastard, son. Your kind heart will be the death of you.'

Half the time I'd only be teasing him. I could kill 1,000 men in front of 1,000 witnesses and Dad would swear I didn't do it. He's a wonderful old bloke, but it's all been too much for him, I'm afraid.

IT SEEMS to me that the modern political scene is bullied and pushed, if not at times controlled, by small lobby groups. They are made up of blinkered people convinced that their single-interest issue is the most important thing in the world.

There are the Greens, Greenpeace, Save the Whales and hundreds of other environmentally friendly, boring groups. You also have various ethnic lobby groups, sex groups, professional interest groups and sundry others. There must be hundreds of whacked-out nutters who have formed their own action factions.

Meanwhile, the Japs are buying every square foot of land they can get hold of and Vietnam has taken over major parts of Australia without firing a shot or digging a single tunnel.

While the greenies are saving our wildlife, forests and waterways, our children are dying in the gutters and back alleys of the nation of drug addiction. While the gay lobby is fighting hard for their political rights, and the various women's groups are kicking up a storm, children are hocking their bums and fannies in the brothels, massage parlours and escort services of the country.

There are plenty of lobby groups prepared to march in the street to save albino water fowl yet no one seems to utter a word of outrage that a generation of Australian children is being destroyed by drugs. No one seems to care about what really matters.

The children of this nation are dying at a faster rate than the bloody trees. Wake up before it is too late.

CHAPTER 15

MINDLESS FILTH
(DIRTY GIRLS
I HAVE KNOWN)

'IF YOU MAKE THE MISTAKE OF FALLING FOR
A PRO, STAB YOURSELF IN THE BACK
STRAIGHT AWAY AND GET IT OVER WITH.'

PROSTITUTES will always be part of the criminal world because they will never be accepted by the people in mainstream society on moral grounds. Legalise the game, call the girls 'sex workers' or whatever you like, but it makes no real difference to what happens on the street and in the parlours. The girls themselves still belong to the underworld.

At best, prostitutes live in a sort of limbo between the legal and the illegal, between night and day and between the criminal world and the normal world. At worst, they're headed for the gutter and an early grave. They are the queens of false pretence – professional pretenders with bedrooms for a stage and their clients for an audience paying for each performance.

They can seem fascinating, exotic creatures but my advice is: Don't ever fall in love with one. Lust, yes. Love, never. If you do make the mistake of falling for a pro, stab yourself in the back straight away and get it over with. Because, believe me, if you don't, then little Miss Tragic Magic will do it for you. And I've seen enough goings on inside and outside massage parlours to know what I'm talking about …

POLISH Suzie went to the same Seventh Day Adventist church as I did, and later we went to the same church school – one of the many I attended. Suzie used to get called 'God's little virgin' by a lot of the other boys. She was so prim and proper and very God-fearing and religious, blushing crimson at the faintest hint of a swear word or a rude joke.

While other girls tried to hike their school uniforms up to turn them into mini-skirts Polish Suzie would wear hers six to eight inches below the knee. She was blue-eyed, peaches-and-cream and oh, so very innocent. Most Seventh Day Adventist girls were on the prim and proper side but little Suzie made the others look almost sinful. Even talking to the boys was a no-no ... a polite hello with eyes looking towards the ground was all we could get out of her.

Later, in her teenage years, after we had both left school, I would sometimes bump into Suzie. She was more talkative but still a real Bible-basher – and she saw me as a truly evil sinner, because I had left the church. She would always tell me, 'I will pray for you, Mark. God loves you.' And off she would go. At 16 years of age she was a tall, well-built girl but she would dress in shoes and socks and long skirts and shirts with buttons all done up. She dressed to make herself look as plain and as unattractive as she could. But you couldn't help noticing that for a Bible-basher she was built in a very wicked, wicked way. In fact, downright sinful. But she didn't act sinful. We were the same age, but she would talk down to me as if I was a naughty little boy and she had Jesus sitting on her shoulder at all times. I always felt guilty whenever I saw her.

A month after I turned 19 in November 1973, I ran into Suzie again. I hadn't seen her for a while, but she bounced up to me full of life to show me her engagement ring. She was dressed in a more 'show off the goodies' manner. She was big and tall and glamorous but still with the innocent face. She told me she was going to marry a sailor – and he wasn't a Seventh Day Adventist, which was a shock.

Suzie was in love, and it had changed her for the better, I thought at the time. She was happy and excited, and as we parted after our short accidental meeting she gave me a quick peck on the cheek. This was most unlike the old Suzie. And there was not a single mention of God, either.

Anyway, about four years later, in 1977, about three months before I got out of H Division in Pentridge, I was in my cell when I was handed a letter. It was from Suzie, telling me she had left her husband and had heard I was in jail. When I got out, she wanted me to ring her at her work at night, as she worked night shifts. She enclosed the phone number and signed off: 'Lots of love and kisses'.

Lots of love and kisses, I thought. She has changed. So when I got out I rang the number and got put on to a chick called Rosie who told me it was a gentlemen's health club and spa. I forget the name of the place now, but it doesn't matter. It took a second for the penny to drop, then I woke up. It was a massage parlor. I asked for Suzie to come to the phone but they said, 'Suzie is with a client'. I was given the address, so I went over and went in. Suzie was in the lounge, having finished with her client. 'Chopper,' she yelled. It was the first time she had used my nickname. I looked at her, and could hardly believe the transformation. God's little virgin had turned into God's great big bloody whore – and proud of it, to boot.

I asked her 'what' and 'why'. She told me that when she lost her cherry she went mad. She wouldn't go into the details of the deep, dark reason for her change of ways. But she took me up into a private room and said: 'Chopper, in the past 12 months I've given more head jobs than a brain surgeon' and laughed at her own joke. I won't go into any details about what happened next, but believe me, God's little virgin had changed her ways indeed.

I went back two, three or four times a week to say hello. Suzie wanted to put me on a sling to look after her, but seeing as she always treated me with Christian kindness whenever she saw me I said 'no'.

Taking money from girls has never been my go. Brothel-owners I don't mind donating to the Chopper Read fund, but not the girls. It never seemed the Aussie thing to do …

Time flies when you're having fun, even if most of it is in Pentridge. I didn't see Polish Suzie again until 1987. By this time she was a big-built woman with a large set of Polish watermelons, and she was big in other ways as well. She now owned and ran her own parlour, and had 21 kids working for her seven days and nights a week, in shifts.

Suzie was now worth a mint. She was married to a Polish Jew who knew a lot about real estate and she owned property all over St Kilda, Elwood and Caulfield. At five foot ten tall and 14 stone there was plenty of her, and she had plenty of money, so I let her give me a small but regular cash sling of $250 a week. That mightn't sound much, but it was a sling – and regular slings from regular places add up. Of course, it was small change to Suzie, but she insisted that I plonk her as well, just for old time's sake. She must have been happy with the service because soon I was on $500 a week – plus Suzie. She could put her own hand inside her mouth – a trick I'd seen before, but only the best could do it.

So there it is. My shy little schoolmate had become a parlour queen. She has two daughters, both going to a good church school. These days she still owns the parlor, but now she has a manageress running the place. She wasn't the first Jesus freak I'd seen having the Devil humped out of her in massage parlours – but she was the only one I'd gone to church with. She would have plenty to put in the collection plate these days. She's richer than most of the so-called rich crooks – pulling in easy $15,000 to $17,000 a week. That takes her out of the basic prostitute league, and makes her a wealthy business woman.

Polish Suzie is one cracker I'll never forget. She once said to me: 'The cops will never pinch a girl who swallows the evidence.' She was a real wisecrack, if ever there was one.

NOW that Margaret and I are no longer together, I can tell a few more stories that would have got me shot before. Previously, I have always maintained that I have never partaken of the sexual delights of either Asian ladies or dark-skinned maidens. My dear old dad would never have approved and, more importantly for my health, Margaret would have considered ways of disposing of my body had she suspected such goings-on. Also, my old 'mates' in the Pentridge chapter of the Ku Klux Klan would have teased me without mercy, and I'm the sensitive sort who doesn't like being made the butt of coarse humour. It makes me cross, and that leads to trouble. But, while on the subject of the 'White is Right' types and Right-wing thinkers in general, very few of them haven't 'banged a monkey' at some stage. Or at least considered it with lustful intention. Men are all sexual hypocrites, and I am no exception, except that I admit it. Which brings me to the point ...

Polish Suzie had a half-Chinese, half-Indian girl working for her named May. May what or who, I don't know, but it wouldn't be her real name anyway. She was a real, brown-skinned beauty – sort of on the buxom side, but graceful. A glamour girl with long black silky hair that flowed down to her arse ... and this dark Chinese face that had porno written all over it. And what an actress. She would go into passionate fits of female pleasure before you even got your pants off. A lot of guys fell in love with May, but you can bet Paris to a French letter she wasn't in love with any of them. May, in fact, according to Suzie was by nature a fish eater, not a meat eater. In other words, she loved girls. The boys were her work, but the 'ladies' were her passion. All of which made me feel a bit foolish, as May had me conned nicely.

May had one small worry – her girlfriend. This was a chick from Bangkok who, in the looks department, made May look downright average. The bombshell from Bangkok was a former bar girl and dancer and whore who married an Aussie, came to Australia, and was promptly put to work in a parlour by her loving husband. This meant she made even less money in Australia than she had in bloody Bangkok because dear hubbie got it all, as he was a partner in the parlour with a well-known Melbourne crim and hoon. May worked at the same parlour, and that was how she came to fall for the Bangkok beauty, whose name was Tina. They ran away together, and Polish Suzie rescued them. They both went to work for Suzie – earning about $2,000 a week each, with another grand apiece going to Suzie. That's $3,000 a week each all up. That's earning power. At $180 an hour, you figure it out.

But Tina and May had a problem. Tina's ex-hubbie wanted her back … and he really wanted to hurt May. He threatened Polish Suzie with a razor blade across the face, which is where I come into the story. Polish Suzie, May and little Tina sat in Suzie's lounge room and told me the whole sad tale. I didn't know the husband, but I did know the peanut, two-bob gangster he was in partnership with in the poxy little parlour they owned in Richmond.

The three ladies were all in tears and quite frightened and really needed my help. I was offered money but, like a gentleman, I declined because I already knew what I wanted. Ha ha. So I agreed to help these damsels in distress. They over-dramatised the whole thing. The husband and the two-bob gangster he was teamed up with took about 45 minutes to find and they didn't even try to fight back. They both got pistol-whipped inside their own parlour in Richmond. I even took the husband back in his car to Suzie's parlour and marched him inside and gave him an extra flogging in front of Tina, May and Polish Suzie, with a warning that if any of the three ladies in question contacted me again in relation to him or any of his tough mates, then I would pull out both his eyes and eat them. I then let him go, and he went very quietly. People get very attached to their eyes.

The girls were impressed, to say the least. And as far as May and Tina were concerned, they couldn't do enough to thank me. If you haven't had a doubleheaded lollipop you haven't lived. May and Tina were a pair of beautiful dirty girls and in 1987, after more than nine years in jail, believe me, I was in no condition to be taking a high moral tone because I had a girlfriend. May and Tina could have got the Pope to surrender without a protest.

And they all lived happily ever after. At least, until Bangkok Tina ran away from May with a drug dealer on a trip to Amsterdam. The dealer returned without her, so I guess it's safe to say Bangkok Tina could be sitting in a window somewhere in Amsterdam. She was a wanton slut, but I'll never forget her. Bless her evil heart.

THERE was this Dutch cracker named Shelley who had once worked in Amsterdam. In Melbourne she didn't work for Polish Suzie, but for another brothel owner in St Kilda. Shelley had a clean and healthy-looking body and fresh-faced looks, but she carried some sort of hepatitis in her blood. So she was a carrier of a deadly disease – and a sexual seductress of the highest order. She would tease them and then please them. Her looks and her hot body drove the mugs mad.

The joke was that whenever the police came into this parlour the boss would always see to it that Shelley took care of them. Which must have been interesting for the policemen's wives because, medically speaking, Shelley was a one-woman plague. I'm glad I never touched her. I'm told she is now HIV positive ... and still working, last I heard. Quite scary.

ON SUNDAY afternoons at a certain hotel in Launceston they put on major cultural events in the beer garden for the more sensitive and artistic souls among the pub clientele. I always considered these events a cultural must. Mainland and local strippers would do their best (and worst) and not a bad afternoon would be had by all. Of particular interest to the patrons was the jelly wrestling and the baby oil wrestling between buxom young ladies wearing G-string bikinis.

This would get very heated, with bikini tops being torn off, and the slip, slap and sliding was fast and furious. The young ladies in question – all being dancers and models, of course – looked fantastic, dripping with baby oil in the sunshine.

Ah, yes, there was plenty to see and do in Launceston. The Satan's Riders motorcycle club imported mainland strippers to put on hot and heated strip shows at their club house, which made the Crown Hotel beer garden affairs look tame. Another popular local pastime among certain sections of Tasmanian society was the 'toss up'. A barrel and barbeque would be put on, attended by a drunken collection of about 20 to 40 louts, crooks and bikies and hillbilly rednecks – and two or three young ladies willing and eager to make friends in a hurry. Hobart might have a university, but there's no doubt Launceston is the cultural hub of Tasmania.

ANYBODY who read my first book would remember the name Tracy Warren … my secret agent in the Dennis Allen camp. She nearly drove Dennis mad by passing on inside information to me. Tracy was always loving and blood loyal. She would do anything for me and proved that over and over again in actions that could have got her killed.

Tracy was a top-looking babe when she had her looks and health, all legs and tits – and false teeth, which is not always a disadvantage in her line of work. She had a crazy sense of humour and a loving nature and was a very sexy woman. She could also fight like a thrashing machine and had a mountain of guts. Dennis Allen once put a gun in her mouth, and she just pulled the barrel out and said, 'Come on, Den. You know that's not what you want to put in my mouth.' Dennis roared laughing. Another time Peter Allen couldn't get the TV to work and Tracy said: 'Hit it with your gun, Peter. That's what you do with everything else.' She got away with murder, playing on a sharp mind, a quick tongue and a lot of rat cunning.

When I stated in the first book that my relationship with Tracy was not sexual, that was a tiny white lie for little Margaret's benefit. I have to admit that when Tracy visited me on contact visits she would swagger up to me, wish me a happy birthday – then proceed to blow the candle out. But it was more an act of Christian kindness and fellowship than anything else, or otherwise I guess I was just an innocent victim of sexual abuse. Ha ha.

Seriously, Tracy was smart and funny and sexy and I thought the world of her – but the heroin kidnapped her. In the end I gave her a choice: the heroin or our friendship. But she wanted both. It broke my heart, but I couldn't handle a junkie. It was totally impossible. It still makes me cry inside.

I still feel sad when I think about Tracy. The heroin won and I lost, and you wonder why I don't like smack dealers. In my mind she will always be a doll – but the junkie's needle broke the doll. Under my heart I have the words tattooed: 'Rest in peace, Tracy Glenda'. I had that tattooed when I said goodbye to Tracy, because in my heart I felt the heroin had killed the girl I knew.

I GUESS it's true to say that I've always had a fascination with strippers – not prostitutes who turn on a strip act five minutes before they turn it on for a gang bang, but the real professional strippers and exotic dancers. I've mentioned before that when I was a young lout, a gang of us went to see a famous American stripper, Alexandra the Great 48. It was a sight I will never forget.

She was wild. Only a short lady – about five foot two – but in high heels she looked magic. Long black hair and a fantastic body. She was a real professional tease – dancing into the crowd, sitting on men's knees, pushing the faces of others between her 48-inch monsters. I sat there watching with my eyes wide open, and my mouth open, and she danced over and bent forward and put her tongue in my mouth. I was embarrassed and shocked. I was only a teenage kid, and no one had ever put their tongue in my mouth before. Yuck. Bloody hell, I thought.

It wasn't the last time I saw Alexandra. She caused a riot when she put on a strip act in Pentridge in the very early '70s. She had agreed to strip only to her G-string, but she went further, and the screws had to close down the show. She pulled the same stunt in Western Australia when she put on a show in Fremantle Prison. She was a sight I will never forget ... the first stripper I'd ever seen and the best by far. She was in her 40s then. I heard she went back to America and married a 17-year-old sailor. She must be an old girl now. I'll never forget her.

Since then I've seen a truckload of so-called strippers, most of them gang bang toss-ups pretending to be Gypsy Rose Lee before they do their come-one, come-all Linda Lovelace impersonation. Some of them were glamorous and magic looking, but in the end a dirty girl is a dirty girl. But the genuine, pure-bred professional stripper and exotic dancer is a wild sight. Probably one of the best I ever saw was a lady named 'Little Egypt'. She was a tall, statuesque professional dancer who was described as an Arabic girl, although I think she was really half Greek and half Egyptian, a reject from a ballet academy because she was too big in the chest.

I went to see her when I was 18 years old. She danced to the Elvis Presley song 'Little Egypt' and my old comrade in arms Cowboy Johnny Harris fell in love and so did I. I thought, What a totally insane-looking woman. The Cowboy and I were front-row regulars from then on at her shows. In her high heels she was at least two inches taller than me, and she had a proud and aloof manner, which should have warned any amorous types in the crowd that it was strictly no touching the merchandise. I saw her pick up an empty glass, break it and open up a guy's face one night after he tried to bite her on the bum. The bouncers dragged the offender out and gave him a sound kicking for his trouble, so the bloke probably wished he'd stayed home that night and taught the budgie to talk instead. But he wasn't the first or the last mug to fall foul of Little Egypt, who was also called the 'Queen of Slice and Dice' because she was so handy with a broken bottle or glass, and would open up your face in flash. But she was fantastic.

I saw Little Egypt many years later selling behind a stall at the Victoria Market. She was a tall, large woman with giant bosoms and even bigger hips – a big mama, but still with a beautiful face like an Egyptian princess. I said, 'Did you used to be a dancer?' She said, 'A hundred years and five children ago. Yeah.'

'Little Egypt?' I said.

'It's Mrs Little Egypt now,' she said. 'Don't tell me ... now I look like the bloody pyramids.' But she was flattered that I should remember her. How could I forget. She was a living fantasy when I was a young man.

Oh, well. One more shattered memory. Ha ha.

PEOPLE on the outside must wonder what really goes on in jail. I must say that all in all there was very little homosexuality in the Victorian prison system. Once in a while you'd get these rampant poofs running through the place, and in the 1970s we had the drag queens in Pentridge – Vicky Litty, Maxine de Barry, Elly May, Wendy McDonald and the rest of the Pentridge Les Girls troupe. But in H Division, where I was, there was none of this decadence. And the AIDS panic later turned a lot of jailhouse queers straight. But A Divison has seen a few famous love stories. There have been some 'Sugar Plum Fairies' dancing their way through that place, believe me. Personally, I find it most distasteful and I enjoy bashing these types as they are a bloody health hazard in a prison and should be stamped out for that reason, if nothing else.

In Geelong Prison in 1984 there was this young bloke who looked like a girl. He was a honey-blond, green-eyed bum boy who worked for a camp escort service on the outside. He was also a mad junkie with a bad habit. The odd thing was that he was married to a young Chinese chick and they had a little baby. The Chinese wife also worked in a massage parlour and the young husband's mum and dad looked after the baby.

I'll call the young guy Danny. Well, Danny boy had to pay for his drugs in jail, and the only way he could do that was by selling his mouth and his bum. Now, he used two to four $50 caps of heroin per day and so he was flat out dropping the soap in the shower to pay his way. It was bloody disgusting, but that was the way he paid his bills. None of this had anything to do with me until Danny boy got himself into real debt, and was a certainty to get himself stabbed. He approached me like a frightened puppy – or should I say 'pussy'– and asked if I'd be willing to speak to people to ask them not to hurt him. In return he offered me his 'services'. I told him he was out of luck, but that I would speak to the people concerned and ask them not to stab him 'too hard'. Ha ha. I laughed and walked away.

Danny boy didn't get stabbed, although he did get bashed pretty badly. About two days after his bashing, his China doll wife came into the prison to see me on a special contact visit on a week day when it was pretty empty. She asked me to help her husband. She had her own drug habit to look after, plus all sorts of money and other troubles, so we worked out a deal. She came to see me once a week on a special contact visit and the screws would turn a blind eye to how friendly she was with me, which was very friendly indeed. Meanwhile, of course, no one got violent with her husband. In jail terms, it was strictly business. And why not? They were only animals, the pair of them. Half the jail was up the husband, so it was only fair that I got the wife. Why should I get left out?

There's a last bit to this story that I consider the height of good humour. One old screw who kept guard on the contact visits spoke to me about the China doll and I told her to 'put a smile on his face' as well. The poor silly old bastard fell in love with the whore and the only way to keep things nice and tidy was to tell her to put an end to the special visits.

Should I feel ashamed? Why? The husband was a sick animal. The wife was a sick slut. Junkies like that are sub-human, pathetic scum. It's sad, but true.

I had the run of Geelong Prison. Frankie Waghorn and I ran the place. But I didn't win any popularity points when I put a virtual overnight stop to homosexual activity in the place – on pain of death – after viewing a TV documentary on AIDS. About a month later, the jail authorities sent me back to Pentridge. Very suspicious.

P.S. Danny boy contracted AIDS in 1990 and was sent to the K Division AIDS unit. The China doll is still hawking herself and at last reports is as healthy as a horse. Thank God.

I'M NOT a great one for tattooed ladies, although Karen's tattoo of me on her back isn't bad, I must admit. Tracy Warren had my name tattooed on her body – 'Property of Chopper'. I've never really seen it, but I've been told about it. Personally I don't really like tattoos on girls. A good-looking chick can wear one or two, I guess, but it just doesn't appeal to me. There was this whore in Melbourne who picked me up and got me back to a motel room. It was a free ride, so I didn't mind, but when she got her gear off she had 'Love me, love my dog' tattooed on her bum. And just over her pussy were the words 'Forsake all hope ye who enter here'. Needless to say I didn't bother getting undressed, and I don't mind saying that I left without partaking. She wasn't ugly, believe me. But the sign-writing dampened my passion. I mean, 'Love me, love my dog' tattooed on her bum. I bet that young lady had a few stories she could tell. The mind boggles.

MY lawyer, Anita Betts, once asked me in anger, 'Who is this Renee Brack?' I said she was a lady who interviewed me for TV – and definitely no dirty girl. I said she was a nice chick 'and a friend'. I gave Anita a pile of mail written to me by Renee to support my numbnut idea that she was a friend.

Anita sat with her head in her hands and looked at me and said, 'Men. You do all your thinking below your belt. You wouldn't know a friend if she bit you on the bum'. I said Renee had never bitten me anywhere, let alone on the bum. 'Well,' said Anita, 'wherever she did bite you, forget it. This woman is not your friend.' Then she showed me Renee's statement to the police and said, 'Little Miss Peaches and Cream Renee Brack is going to be a Crown witness against you'.

I said, 'No, no. She will be okay. She's on my side.'

'She'll be okay, all right,' yelled Anita. 'When she gets in the witness box I'll tear her apart.'

One letter in particular written to me by Renee gave Anita reason to crack a somewhat evil smile. 'Wait 'til I toss this at her,' she said. 'No, no,' I protested. 'I don't want you to rip it into Renee.'

'Chopper,' Anita said. 'You're a nice bloke. But when it comes to women like Renee Brack let me do the thinking.' A week later Anita visited me in Risdon with the *Truth* newspaper under her arm. On the front page was Renee proudly telling one and all that she was to be called as a Crown witness against me.

Margaret had warned me that Renee Brack was trying to climb her own personal ladder at my expense, but as usual I disagreed. Renee continued to write to me, but her letters seemed to take a slight turn, pressing me for info on this, that and the other, and telling me of her ideas for a book of her own, of her hopes to be a writer. She went on about how the interview she did with me had gone to America 'as I told you it would' and that when I had told her that the interview with me wouldn't do her career any harm, I had been right, and wouldn't it be wonderful if we could do a second interview. Rah, rah, rah, blah, blah, blah.

Still convinced Renee was a top chick and a friend, I gave her a wrap in my second book – much to her delight. All was well until an article appeared on the front page of *Truth* again, explaining that Chopper was in love with a beautiful TV reporter named Renee Brack, and quoting her as saying that I was bombarding her with mail. I was made to look like a lovesick mental case.

My so-called friendship with Renee Brack had turned into the balcony scene from *Romeo and Juliet*. Anita came in to see me with the article. 'Well,' she said, 'what do you think of your girlfriend, now? She is not your friend, Mark. She is a TV reporter, and you're Chopper Read.'

I said, 'What do you mean?' She said: 'Mark, you poor simple soul, in the world of television it's self, self, self. There is no friendship.' And she said a few other things which we won't repeat here. At last the penny dropped. The article in the *Woman's Day* where Renee explained she was not terribly comfortable with the attention and did not enjoy the idea of being the pin-up girl for some guy in prison, made it clear to me. As always, Anita and my faithful girlfriend Margaret were right and I was wrong.

That wonderful little article in *Woman's Day* claiming Renee was my 'pin-up girl' caused Margaret to really spit the dummy with me. When Renee had been in Launceston I didn't come home on the Saturday night and Margaret suspected that I had been up to no good, and furthermore, she suspected that the no good I was up to was Renee Brack.

My pleas of 'not guilty' fell on deaf ears and the various stories that followed in the newspapers and magazines quoting Renee and hinting that I was sweet on her were the last straw for Margaret in a haystack full of past bugger-ups on my part. So Margaret went her own way.

In spite of Renee's continued letters to me I accepted the fact that I had been in serious error to believe that I had a friend in Renee. Another article in *Australian Penthouse* called 'Chopper's World' written by Renee Brack simply proved to me that she seemed to be basing her career on the fact that she had once interviewed a man with no ears ... turning a bowl of porridge into a six-course meal, if you get my meaning.

Renee tried to have it both ways in the stories she did. She tried to distance herself from me – but made it look as if I was mad keen on her. But let me tell you there was none of this shy stuff when she was over in Tassie shooting the TV interview with me.

I don't know what it is about ladies and guns, but there is a definite psychological effect when you mix the two. They get an excited gleam in their eyes and just blast away as if there's no tomorrow. And when the clip is empty they want to do it again. Renee Brack was a classic example of this. At first she was like a timid little kitten – frightened, yet fascinated – but when I put my Beretta in her hand and told her to pull the trigger she was scared at first but when she pulled the trigger and the blast hit her ear drums she said, 'Shit, this is great' and blasted away.

Off camera she must have punched 50 to 100 rounds out of that Beretta and the gleam in her eye told me was rapt. She had never fired a gun before, and here she was in the bush after a session in the pub blowing the hell out of anything she could aim at.

When she fired the .357 magnum, the noise of the blast nearly deafened her and the recoil made it buck in her hands, but she still punched six shots out of it. In spite of herself, in spite of her efforts to maintain a cool and professional attitude, she was like a little kid in a lolly shop.

The camera crew took turns blowing the hell out of anything and everything, and Renee led the charge. Renee had her own personal camera with her, and we took about 20 personal photos of her in various poses with the guns. She is a former model and knows how to bung it on for the camera. I said I wanted copies of all the photos, especially the ones of her and me together, but she wrote to me in jail later telling me that none of them had turned out!

I think she was a bit worried that some of them might turn up in my book. When Renee and I said goodbye to each other in the bar of the Clarendon Arms Hotel in Evandale she jumped up and threw her arms around me like a little schoolgirl and gave me a hug and a big sloppy kiss in front of the whole bar and TV crew. I gave her my Zippo solid brass cigarette lighter engraved 'Mark Brandon Read 1000W', and when they drove away I foolishly thought that I had found a new friend.

In the *Penthouse* article Renee mentioned about me giving her the cigarette lighter. Margaret had always wondered where the bloody lighter had got to. Then the article went on to talk about how Renee and I had enjoyed a quiet breakfast alone at which she said I 'confessed' to having killed two or three men before I'd even had sex for the first time.

Margaret really loved that little lot! What was I doing having breakfast with Renee Brack? And when you deny something to one woman in relation to another woman they find you guilty without the benefit of a trial. An angry, suspicious female has no mercy.

Human nature being what it is, Margaret was not the only one to suggest I had in fact got up to no good with the lovely Renee, and all my heartfelt denials only confirmed my 'guilt' in the minds of the suspicious. They all thought I was either trying to save my own neck or attempting to be a 'gentleman'. It's a no-win situation, and it's no use Renee telling Margaret or anyone else that nothing took place. But these little comments from Renee in these nitwit articles don't help my 'not guilty' plea one bit.

The truth is this: I swear on my gunsmith's wooden leg that I never did no hanky panky with Renee Brack, and that is a very solemn oath indeed. You ask her and she will tell you. Look at me: no ears, half my teeth missing and with more scars than Frankenstein.

Anyway, the next chick who interviews me will have to be pig ugly – with no five-hour piss-ups, no physical touching, no drives up bush tracks for drunken shoot 'em ups, no quiet breakfasts together, and definitely no engraved cigarette lighters as goodbye gifts.

Bloody Renee Brack. While it is true she is a magic-looking little chick with a heap of dash, guts and personality she isn't my friend and never was.

But all that to one side, I don't hate Renee. She's just a sharp chick looking to kick on in her chosen field, and I hope her interview with me and the various stories she's handed out to magazines and newspapers on her 'Chopper Read adventure' all help her climb up that greasy pole. And one day when she steps up to collect her Logie and gives her 'I'd like to thank my producer' speech, people will say, 'Yeah, baby. Him and Chopper Read as well'.

Ha ha ha.

CHAPTER 16

MURDER, MAYHEM AND MADMEN

'I PUT ONE ROUND THROUGH HIS HEAD.
IT TOOK OFF HIS NOSE AND THE BACK
OF HIS SKULL …'

THIS is the story of the late 'Donkey Dick'. I can't tell you where this happened, when it happened, what year or even what state, as the idiot in question is on the missing list, and the police are wondering where he is and how he got there.

Now, this character was stronger than 10 fat ladies, faster than a Saturday night rapist and able to jump tall girls in a single bound. We called him Donkey Dick. He was a bit of a would-be tough guy and a dope grower and dealer and a shocking mistreater of females. He was none of my concern until he raped the wife of a friend of mine. She was, or is, a nice chick with a lovely, kind nature. But with a few drinks in her she became a full-on, out-of-control tease and a bloody embarrassment. But even so, raping her is not on. I don't agree with that sort of bullshit. No one needs to rape anyone.

Anyway, my mate, the husband of the rape victim, and myself went to see Donkey Dick. I took my gun as always, planning to give the offender a good beating and pistol-whipping and kicking to help give him a little attitude readjustment.

We got to Donkey's farmhouse and found him in the garage. He had a very cocky attitude and got smartmouthed with my mate – calling his good lady wife a moll and a toss-up. A fight started and my mate asked me to stay out of it. So I did. It lasted about five minutes, with my mate being done like a dinner. Then Donkey Dick made a strategic error of judgement. He turned towards me and screamed, 'Come on. Do you want some as well?' So I pulled out my handgun (I won't mention the precise make and model) and put one round through his head. It took off his nose and the back of his skull, as I was using ammo called 'wad cutters'.

I don't know where Donkey is buried, as my mate saw to the departure details, but I'm told he will never be found as he is in fertiliser heaven. I did not intend to shoot Donkey, but these things happen in even the best circles. Anyway, he was a sex offender. He got his right whack. Bugger him.

HORATIO Morris used to tell a story of a gunfight on the Melbourne waterfront back in the '50s. Horatio was armed with a five-shot Colt revolver and was chasing another gunman in a running battle.

Horatio put five shots into the back of the fleeing gunman, yet the injured man didn't slow at all. Morris had to re-load at a flat out gallop, as he had to kill this one. A wounding would not be enough. It was a Dockies' dispute that had to be solved the permanent way.

Horatio re-loaded and continued after his potential Stawell Gift winner. He fired another five shots, all hitting the mark in the back and the neck. The wounded man finally tripped over. Horatio was out of ammo and had to finish the fellow off with a half a dozen blows to the head with a length of iron pipe. Amazing … 10 slugs in him and he was still alive and breathing.

Horatio figured the bloke had run about a thousand yards with 10 slugs in his back, and he only fell at the finish because he lost his footing and tripped over. The fellow was disposed of in the backyard of a house in Newport.

This was a shooting story that Horatio treated as a medical lesson. I've used a .32 calibre revolver myself and a .32 calibre automatic, and I can also state that unless you hit them in the head with the slug, you'd be better off to pistol-whip them with the gun itself. These .32s may look pretty, but they have no stopping power.

It is interesting that most gunmen, myself included, soon learn to take an interest in matters medical. The human body is a tough thing and if you want to fix it, like a doctor, or hurt it, like a toe-cutter, you have to know what you are doing. Each profession takes skill, although it is a little hard to bulk bill as a standover man. When I shot Chris Liapis in Footscray, I used a Beretta .32 calibre automatic. The bullet went in his guts and the doctors found it in his underpants when he got to hospital. It had passed out his bottom. Amazing.

I shot another bloke in Canton in the neck with a .22 calibre revolver. He coughed the slug up and spat it out as he ran away. Talk about spitting chips.

When using the small calibre weapons, you take a big risk. I have heard of a .22 slug ricocheting off a bloke's false teeth from a handgun held only a foot away from his mouth. How embarrassing. But that is the risk that you take when using .22 and .32 calibre handguns. With gear like that it has to be in the brain via the earhole to be 100 per cent sure, otherwise you're just wasting your time.

In late 1973, Cowboy Johnny Harris was involved in a fight with a member of the Coffin Cheaters motorcycle gang. The bikie was wearing a full face helmet, which made fighting rather hard if you were tossing punches at the head.

I fired a shot from a sawn-off .22 rifle in the face of the bikie, which didn't even crack the protective shield of the helmet, although it sure scared the shit out of him as he ran for his bike. As he hopped on board, I fired a second shot which hit the back of his helmet. I doubt whether he even got a headache out of the whole episode.

I know I talk about guns a lot, but I get great pleasure from them. They are my tools of trade, but they are also my hobby. I must confess, although it is not much of a secret, that I do enjoy shooting a total arsewipe. But I did not shoot Sid Collins. If I had done so, rest assured, dear reader, I would have shot him several times for the sheer delight of watching him squirm with pain and fear.

A bullet is the one thing which brings a man back to his real self. A truly hard man will remain hard, even after being shot. He will look you in the eye and say, do your worst. I've met a few tough bastards, but believe me, they are rare.

Just because a man has a few tattoos, a criminal record and a love of blood doesn't make him a hard man. There are some real weak men who hide their cowardice behind a gun and a tough image. And there are honest quiet men who, when pushed, have a touch of steel in their spines.

Most so-called tough guys will cry and panic and get this pathetic childlike look when death stares them in the face. They plead and beg and whimper like puppies. They beg and cry for you to spare them.

It is then that you see the real person behind the false face. I love it.

I WAS having a drink with Mad Archie, Garry the Greek and half a dozen other local gun-toting ratbags in a nightclub in St Kilda. It was 7 April 1974. Why do I remember the date? I'll tell you. Mad Charlie took out a small gun and tapped it on the bar and called for silence. After about 60 seconds there was silence – enough for Mad Charlie to speak. He said, 'Does anyone know what day it is?' No one knew what he meant. 'It's the seventh of April,' said Charlie. 'Crazy Joe Gallo got shot on the seventh of April 1972, outside Umberto's Clamhouse on Mulberry Street, Brooklyn, in New York on this day two years ago … and I think a moment of silence is called for.'

After an insane moment of comical silence Mad Archie turned to me and said: 'Who the hell is Crazy Joe Gallo?' Mad Charlie nearly had a tear in his eye by this stage. He was bloody well named. A minute of silence for the memory of Crazy Joe Gallo, if you don't mind! Charlie lived in his own magic world. But we loved him, bless his comic-book gangster heart. And, as I said in my first book, there is still a handful of nutters around with more guns than God who love Charlie. Even though Charlie and I have gone our separate ways I still have a soft spot for 'The Don', as we called him.

What a lot of people in the Australian crime scene don't understand is that Charlie could still muster a crew of headbanging mental cases armed to the arse in no time flat. If Charlie made the phone call, Dave the Jew would still take his side. Mad Archie, who is genuinely insane, would go in with Charlie, and I could easily name a dozen more who now live in a sort of semi-retirement ever since the blood war they dreamed of never happened. We all looked to Charlie as the man who could start it – and the truth is, he still could. His old crew would launch a bloodbath for the sheer hell of it. In our hearts Mad Charlie, 'the Godfather of Giggles', will always be the Don. Crazy but true.

JIMMY the Tooth was a raving nutter. An old mate of my dear friend Vincent Villeroy, he was a crazy pom from London's east end. He lived in Port Melbourne and was a seaman. He was a tough bastard. I once saw him win a $100 bet in a pub by pulling out his own front tooth with a pair of pliers. He was quicker than any dentist – it took him about 30 seconds, but there was a lot of blood involved. Where do you see that sort of stuff in today's la-de-da world?

We once brought Jimmy along with us on a torture job. He was supposed to grab the victim and get him into the car, but he beat him nearly to death in the street and pinched his watch. You couldn't say Jimmy was a big thinker. That was the last time we used him as muscle. He was a bloody mental case.

IN 1974 I met a nice young kid called Kenny Knight. He had a touch of the tar brush in him – I think he was quarter Aboriginal – and he had a lot of guts and plenty of dash and style. He was a sharpie, and would follow me around looking for a good time. He was a violent young crook, and not a bad little fighter. He would do anything for me. But he was another one who was dancing on the edge of the drug world. I pulled him out of it while I was around. I was attacked once in the Woolshed Bar of the Australia Hotel in Melbourne, and while I was ripping my thumbs in and out of the eye sockets of my attacker, young Kenny sliced the offender's neck open with a broken beer glass.

When Kenny went to jail, the silly young bugger got into glue sniffing and died with his head in a plastic bag sniffing glue in his cell in 1975. He was a good kid and it was a sad, stupid waste. He was a top young bloke with a heart of gold, and he looked up to me and I wished I could have saved him. If I don't mention him here, he will never get a mention anywhere.

TOMMY Hodges was another young crim who looked up to me ever since we were teenage kids. He wasn't a very violent bloke, but he was a gutsy thief and a shifty crook who could keep his mouth shut when it mattered. Tommy saw me stab another crim in the head with a screwdriver. The victim couldn't tell on me – he was alive, but half a veggie. Tommy got questioned over the matter, and I mean 'questioned' in a vigorous manner, but he stuck solid and didn't say anything. He mightn't have been violent himself but he was a hard young bloke and he could take a flogging and say nothing, which is a special brand of toughness. He never mentioned my name in connection with the screwdriver incident or anything else, and saved me a lot of legal bother. Tommy also died with a plastic bag of glue over his head in a prison cell in the late 1970s. Don't ask me why. Another stupid waste.

LLOYD Fenner is another name I've mentioned in the other books. He was one of the true hard men I'd met in my life, and I've met a lot who thought they were hard. Old Lloyd is dead now. He was a fisherman. I wouldn't call him a criminal, but his fishing boat had taken a few big-name crooks to sea for their last goodbye during the dockies' wars. When I smashed Jack Twist over the head with a pool cue in the Mornington pub when I was a young bloke, it was Lloyd Fenner who saved my neck by getting me out of the joint before Twist worked out what had happened and who had done it. Lloyd was a good mate of my uncle Eddy Miller, which was why he looked after me on that occasion. He was a legend on the Melbourne waterfront and in the Victorian fishing industry and a man I greatly admired. I was sad when he died. The story goes that he once put a man in a scallop cage, cut the body open and dropped the cage over the side of the boat in Port Phillip Bay. He was not a man to be trifled with. Take my word for it.

ANDY is a mate of mine in Launceston. He is a nice, polite, friendly, easy-going sort of chap, kindhearted and with a generous way about him, and a lot of loyalty towards me. He also has a plate in his head and gets a bit funny when he has a few drinks in him.

One night at a barbeque at my place I was showing Andy a .38 calibre automatic handgun. He was rapt. We had a few friendly gatecrashers from up the road arrive, but Andy didn't like one of them. He put the .38 to the bloke's head and tried to pull the trigger. The weapon was unloaded and Andy didn't really know how to work an automatic handgun even if it had been loaded. Everyone there thought Andy was joking, but I saw by the look on his face that he was serious. Dead serious, you could say.

Andy later joined us in the 'hole-in-the-head' shooting club, and he proved a very dangerous man indeed. When he was handed an SKK 7.62 mm assault rifle with a 30-round clip when he was half pissed he started shooting at anything that moved – including some club members in the bush that Andy thought were wild animals. (In fact, they were wild animals – but not the furry sort Andy thought.)

Andy was a dead set menace. He would hang the SKK out the car window and take pot shots as we drove along. But for all his madness he was a bloody good bloke and very true to his word. His older brother Shane is in Risdon, doing the big one for murder – in fact, two murders. I see Shane as an otherwise good bloke who just had a bad day which took a slight turn for the worse and resulted in a fatal falling out. He is a happy-go-lucky, easy-going fellow. Most killers are easygoing, so I've noticed. You'll find very few bad-tempered murderers. The average murderer has only ever lost his temper once – resulting in the death of another person. But I stress that is the average murderer. Men who are forced to kill or be killed in the criminal world are another story, as what they do isn't real murder. It is simply the way it is and the way it has to go … kill or be killed is not murder in my book.

THE best kick boxer ever to step foot in Pentridge as an inmate was George Zacharia, a middleweight who was ranked third in the world ratings. I used to spar with him in 1985, and let me tell you, this bloke could fight. He was the hardest man I'd ever put the gloves on with. He would hit me 20 times to my six punches. He wasn't allowed to kick or he would have killed me. But as a puncher he was bloody dangerous enough, never mind the feet. A student of the Bob Jones karate style, George was deadly, yet he could never make me walk backwards. I would just march forward in on him while he punched my head in. He hit me with a punch one time that I'm sure exploded 10 per cent of whatever brain cells I have left. But with the gloves off George was a gentle-natured man and a bloody good bloke. I couldn't mention kick boxing without paying tribute to George Zacharia – the best I've ever been in the same ring with. Thank God it was only sparring.

Talking of kick boxing, they used to put on contests in Pentridge in 1991. Big Davey Hedgecock, a former world-ranked kick boxer on his way to a world title before some scallywag shot him in the shoulder, used to bring in a team of professional kick boxers to fight the team of ex-professional kick boxers doing time.

Dave Hedgecock is a legend in the Melbourne nightclub scene. He runs a security company that supplies bouncers to clubs and pubs and discos all over town. Dave is a very good friend of my old jail mate Frankie Waghorn. He is also a friend of a gentleman in Lygon Street, Carlton, who doesn't like me much, but that's not Dave's fault.

Anyway, back to the story of the boxing shows. Being the charitable, goodhearted fellow he is, Dave arranged to bring a few strippers into Pentridge with the boxing shows. Wearing as little as legally allowed, they would jump into the ring between rounds and hold up cards indicating which round it was, and strut their stuff – much to the delight of the crowd. The whole thing was videoed and replayed throughout the jail and, believe me, the between-rounds entertainment put on by the girls was the main attraction. The girls knew it, and played up to the crowd and to the camera.

The powers that be ended up stopping these boxing and girl shows. Sometimes, the jail authorities have no sense of humour at all.

CHAPTER 17

THE COUCH POTATOES

The question of whether Mark Brandon Read is mad or bad has been discussed by police, underworld figures, lawyers and several juries. But the real answer about Read's state of mind requires experts. Here three of them give their opinion.

2 November 1992.

Dear Ms Betts,

Re: Mark Read.

I interviewed your client at the Risdon Prison Special Unit on 31 October 1992. To assist me with my assessment I was provided with a copy of Mr Read's Record of Prior Convictions.

Mark Read is a 37-year-old man who, prior to his

arrest, was living in a de facto relationship in Newnham. He had previously been released from prison in November 1991, and remained free until May 1992. He has recently been convicted of charges arising out of the shooting of one Sidney Collins.

Mr Read has a most interesting family background. He was the older of two children of a family that lived mainly in Victoria. His father served with the Regular Army for 26 years and at the time of retirement from the forces was a senior NCO. Mr Read's mother had previously been the matron of a Seventh Day Adventist Missionary College in New Zealand. Mr Read's father's occupation led to the household having many moves both within Victoria, and to other states. Your client estimates that as a result of these moves he would have attended approximately 20 schools. This caused him to have limited opportunities to form any enduring friendships.

His difficulty in peer relationships was exacerbated by the household's religious practices. As noted above, Mr Read's mother had been a matron of a Seventh Day Adventist College. She was a strict adherent of this faith, and Mr Read's father was required to convert to the same faith. The household followed Seventh Day Adventist principles which included fundamentalist religious views, strict observance of a Saturday Sabbath, vegetarianism and asceticism. There were prohibitions upon the use of alcohol and drugs, and the expression of aggression. Corporal punishment was frequent, with a 'Spare the rod, spoil the child' philosophy prominent.

This religious background caused your client to be further isolated from his peers, and subject to some schoolyard bullying and harassment. Furthermore, the observance of a Saturday Sabbath meant that, despite his increasingly powerful build, he was unable to participate in various sporting activities.

Once a child emerges from such a background and moves into adolescence, there is a fundamental choice as to whether to accept the household's rules for living, or repudiate them. There is no middle ground. Mr Read rejected his mother's upbringing and her church, and during his adolescence became increasingly difficult to control. In contrast, his sister embraced maternal values and fundamentalist religion. Mr Read left the Seventh Day Adventist Church when he was aged 15. Interestingly, his father left the church not long after, and the parental marriage subsequently failed.

Mr Read left school, and obtained work readily. His athletic physique allowed him to work as a nightclub bouncer from a relatively young age. In such a way, having left the household culture he entered a new sub-culture, the criminal underworld of Melbourne. He became involved in many acts of violence, the majority which appear to have been directed at other criminal elements. His modus operandi evolved into 'standing over' other criminals such as drug dealers and massage parlor operators. He appears to have not been a particularly successful criminal, having spent the period 1974–91 almost continuously in custody.

His most notorious offence was the armed abduction of a County Court judge in 1978. This was the only offence about which he has expressed any remorse or regret. He told me that all the other offences had been against criminal elements, but he had no personal wish to harm the judge. When he later discovered that the judge had recently recovered from cardiac surgery, your client wrote to him, apparently to apologise. Mr Read told me that he and the judge, who had by then retired, subsequently exchanged correspondence.

I was interested to learn of the background to Mr Read having mutilated his ears, the basis for his nickname, 'Chopper'. He told me that he had been directed by the Prison Classification Committee to spend his time in Pentridge's H Division, and that he had been informed that he would be there for a long time. He gave me a vivid account of H Division and its inmates, many of whom are mentally disturbed or show markedly disorganised behaviour. Mr Read assured prison authorities that he would be getting out of H Division; they replied that he would not. He then resolved to win the day by doing something so out of the ordinary the authorities would feel obliged to transfer him. He persuaded another prisoner to cut his ears off with a razor blade. He was apparently moved out of H Division promptly. He denied any other acts of mutilation. He advised me that his behaviour prompted a virtual epidemic of ear cutting within H Division as other prisoners tried the same ploy. Mr Read told me that this group of prisoners were nicknamed the Van Gogh Club, with Mr Read the unofficial president. Although there have been no other acts of mutilation, Mr Read is covered in a large array of amateur tattoos, most of which have a theme of violence or bravado.

Although Mr Read has been a singularly violent person, his repudiation of maternal values does not appear to be complete. For example, he denied any significant alcohol or substance abuse, and expressed almost moralistic views concerning those who profited from drug abuse. He had no regrets about his offences against drug dealers and underworld figures.

His past health, other than for injuries, has been good. He has incurred several injuries which might be regarded as an occupational hazard, e.g. hit on the head with a hammer when aged 18, shot in the back when 16, and so on. There is no history of psychiatric assessment, although he had spoken briefly with Dr Bartholomew, a Victorian Forensic Psychiatrist, while he was in Pentridge.

During the interview, despite his somewhat fearsome appearance, Mr Read presented in a manner that might be described as friendly and charming. He was articulate and seemed to be above average intelligence. He was very plausible. There was no evidence of any mood disturbance of thought, perception or cognition.

COMMENT

THERE is no evidence of psychiatric disorder in Mr Read. He clearly has a most unusual personality, but then, that would be expected of someone who is not uncomfortable about being regarded as a professional criminal. I had wondered whether an anti-social personality disorder can be diagnosed in this man, and technically it probably can. However, typical features such as alcohol and drug abuse or impulsivity were not present. While he clearly has been violent on many occasions, I gained the impression of a man who has control over aggression, rather than being violent in a chaotic or disorganised manner. From a psychiatric perspective, there was no disorder present which would suggest any particular propensity for him to lose control of his aggressive impulses.

My report has to be somewhat qualified by the lack of third party information. This report relied on information provided by Mr Read, and his Record of Prior Convictions. Ideally, one would have liked to have information from Victorian authorities before reaching diagnostic conclusions.

In conclusion, on the information available, I could discern no formal psychiatric disorder in your client. He may satisfy the criteria for diagnosis of an anti-social personality disorder, but this is not a mental illness. This personality diagnosis is probably more appropriate for his younger days. An impression is gained of some mellowing in recent years. While the presence of such a personality is generally associated with violent behaviour, with respect to your client I gained the impression that his violence has been controlled or utilised, rather than being chaotic or disorganised. In other words, if he acts in a violent manner, he has control and choice over this.

Please do not hesitate to contact me for any further information or clarification.

Yours faithfully,
Ian Sale FRANZCP

Director of Public Prosecutions, 2 November 1992
Office of Director of Public Prosecutions
c/- The Department of Justice
15 Murray Street
Hobart.

Dear Sir

Re: The Queen v Mark Brandon Read.

At your request I examined the above at the Special Institution on 20 October 1992 and again on 29 October 1992. I have studied the Crown Papers and I have also obtained a psychological assessment to determine his personality profile.

Mr Read was quite co-operative at the interview and agreed to do the psychological test, the results of which I shall incorporate in the report.

I did contact Pentridge jail on two occasions but was unable to get any information as to any psychiatric assessments while Mr Read was incarcerated there. He tells me he did see Dr A. Bartholomew, but it was only for chats and not formally as a patient.

Mr Read did not admit to the offence nor was he vociferous denying it. He did say that there was a lot he could say at the trial on his behalf, particularly in relation to the circumstances of the shooting but he was in a 'Catch 22' situation and whatever he said would have been misinterpreted, particularly because of the notorious publicity he received at the time he published his book and the attendant TV and news coverage.

BACKGROUND HISTORY

MR READ was born in Carlton, Victoria, older of the two children. His father was in the regular army and both he and his mother were in their 30s when they married. His mother was a very devout Seventh Day Adventist and he tells me he spent the first 18 months of his life in a baby home because his mother could not look after him because of some nervous problem. As he was growing up his mother got his father to punish him as soon as he came home from work and quite often for no good reason. She used to wait for him to come home and his father thrashed him using the army webbing, thick canvas belt.

At school he was regarded as dyslexic and at one stage the school counsellor labelled him as autistic. He was bullied at school and, as it was drummed into him that he should 'turn the other cheek', there was not much he could do about it. He did get into trouble at school and on one occasion he received 15 straps on his hand but he felt that it was what he deserved.

His parents used to argue a lot but there was no physical violence between them. The worst arguments were regarding the Seventh Day Adventist religious tenets. He was made a ward of the state at 14 years and a year later he left home. His father finally left his mother and has lived on his own ever since.

When he was about 16 years they moved from a rather rough neighbourhood to Prahran where, apparently, 'well-respected' criminals live, and he began associating with the sons of the Painters and Dockers and he feels that is where he started going wrong and that is the first time he actually saw a .32 calibre hand gun.

His first relationship with a female was when he was 18 but he was cautious about relationships as his father had given him a very graphic picture of the horrors of VD and the treatment where an 'umbrella-like' contraption was inserted in the urethra to scrape the infection!

He admits that he first went to jail at the age of 17 years and by the age of 20 years he received his first long sentence of 3½ years and this was for trying to rob a massage parlour. It was during this incarceration in H Division that he could not handle the jail and cut his ears off so that he could get out of the yard. He has spent a total of about 18 years in jail since age 20 years, with only a few months out on parole each time.

The last offence was when he took a judge hostage and this was to obtain the release of a friend to whom he had given his word that he would get out.

He has had one relationship with a Margaret for the past 10 years. She still stands by him.

Although he drinks, occasionally a bit too much, he has never used drugs and appears to be excessively critical of drug peddlers. He claims he came to Tasmania to get away from the criminal element and he is sorry that he ever got involved in the present situation.

On clinical examination Mr Read comes over as an intelligent and charming man. He is self-conscious about his ears and his heavily tattooed body. Most of these tattoos were put on when he was about 20 years old. He has tried to remove some of them.

I could find no evidence of psychiatric disorder. His personality testing shows anti-social traits which is not surprising, considering his background and the amount

Above: The pro-gun lobby … God help us all.

Below: One of these men is a dangerous psychopath. John Silvester aiding and abetting my literary efforts in Pentridge.

A shout-out to the ladies … *Above left:* Tracee … number one fan. *Above right:* Desiree and my god daughter Gemma. *Below*: Mary-Ann from the Tax Department with her pussy.

Above left: Tauree … my favourite female writer. *Above right*: The White Dove … would require more than a single shot. *Below left*: Kerry … the t-shirt is a collector's item. *Below right*: Don't send any hacksaws, just a better cardigan.

To Mark
"The Chopper"
Read. Wishes
Love & Best Wishes
from your friend
Sherrie
Sinatra
xx x

Sherrie Sinatra, Australia's greatest lady wrestler. Her scissor hold is a killer.

Me and television reporter Renee Brack … it was only business.

Above: My legal team: Anita Betts (*front*), Peter Warmbrunn and Narelle McConnon.

Below left: Keeping it in the family, Tassie-style: My barrister Greg Richardson – Anita's ex-husband and (*right*) Anita, robed for battle.

Russell Street bombing, March 1986. My good friend Craig 'Slim' Minogue maintains his innocence.

Above: Sid (*left*) … maybe he shot himself

Below left: Rocky Devine and me.

Below right: I'm a rugby convert. I've always liked mindless violence.

of time he has spent in jail. He is in many ways immature, which is demonstrated by his somewhat childish 'show off' bravado expressions. In many ways he is his own worst enemy.

OPINION

Mr Read is not suffering from a clinical mental illness, at least I cannot find psychiatric indication for him to be considered a dangerous criminal. However, there is some evidence that his alcohol abuse has been a disinhibiting effect, which releases some of his impulsive behaviour which he appears to have good control of when sober.

Yours Sincerely,
Dr W P Lopes
M.B.B.S., D.C.IHI., D.P.M.,
M.R.C.Psych (U.K.) M.P.I.HI. & T.M. (U.S.A.)
Senior Forensic Psychiatrist.

....

Mr Irons   *14 October 1977.*
Probation Officer,
Probation and Parole Division
55 Swanston Street,
Melbourne 3000

Dear Mr Irons,

Re: Mr Mark Brandon Read.
This note just confirms our conversation last evening when we decided that Mr Read was not a suitable person for psychiatric management and accordingly I am not offering him further appointments.

I think that it is likely that he will fall foul of the law again and I would have thought that there is little anybody can do to alter his lifestyle. I note from his case records that when his release was being planned he was not motivated to engage in any therapeutic alliance with a psychiatrist.

Yours sincerely,
Dr W. C. Canning
Consulting Forensic Psychiatrist.

CHAPTER 18

THE SECRET READ FILES

'REASON FOR TRANSFER: READ HAS BEEN STANDING OVER OTHER PRISONERS'

FOR police, parole officers and the Office of Corrections, Mark Read has been a pain in the neck for almost three decades. Bureaucrats from several departments have been kept busy documenting Read's activities, both inside and outside jail. For the first time these confidential official documents have been released through the Freedom of Information Act.

They give a fascinating insight into the uneasy truce Read has maintained with officialdom for most of his many years behind bars.

Reading between the lines reveals a maverick prisoner who, for all his well-earned reputation as a violent stand-over man, keeps up an almost jocular relationship with his keepers, the Parole Board and police. This reflects the mildly astonishing fact that apart from minor teenage scrapes – and the inspired stupidity of attempting to kidnap Judge Martin in his own courtroom – Read has not only never been found guilty of harming innocent members of the public but also the traditional enemies of the underworld, police and prison officers.

From start to finish, the cheeky vernacular style which has made Read

Australia's most unlikely best-selling author shines through the stilted jargon of official correspondence.

27 June 1975

Transfer details:
Read, Mark, to H Division.
Reason for Transfer:
Read has been standing over other prisoners.

11 April 1977

I request to be transferred into One Yard for protection because there are prisoners in this Division that firmly believe that I bashed Bobby Barron on behalf of the prison officers. This is not true, but it is a very hard thing to disprove. I am not doing long enough to warrant getting into any more trouble. Thank you.

  If you decide to send me to another jail, I would like to go to Sale.

  Mark Brandon Read.

Comments.

Read has proved to be a standover type, his application is not recommended.

12 July 1977

To Mr H Poden, Parole officer, Head Office.
Memorandum.
Mark Read.
File No 74/4480.

The above named is scheduled to be released on parole some time next August and you have been assigned as his parole officer. The file is at head office with administration and it may be wise for you to look at it before he is actually released.

It would be appreciated if you could attach the enclosed correspondence to his and note that the father's address has been changed.

Best of British luck.

R H Perch.

RELEASED FROM JAIL 1977

26 January 1978

DIRECTOR-GENERAL.

Mr Nick Doyle, Division of Correctional Services, phoned at 11 am today to advise that he had just been informed that a Mr Mark Read, a prisoner on bail, had entered a County Court and threatened Mr Justice Martin with a shotgun. Mr Read is being held in the County Court cells and is being questioned by police. It is not known who overpowered Mr Read. As soon as more information is to hand Mr Doyle will communicate it.

A S Cox,
Acting Secretary.
Minister: for your information.

Incident at Melbourne County Court on Thursday,
January 26, 1978, at 10.25am.
Read, Mark Brandon.

Released on parole from Pentridge on 12 August 1977.

Mark Read entered the fifth court on the sixth floor of
the County Court building in Melbourne.

Judge Martin was hearing Crown Appeals. Prison
officers Leonard and McCurry were in attendance.

Mark Read walked through the court to the judge's
bench, he produced a gun and held it to the judge's head.
He indicated to the judge that he was going to take him
hostage to obtain the release of James Loughnan.

James Richard Loughnan was certified and
transferred from Pentridge to Ararat Mental Hospital on
16 December 1977. Loughnan sent a threatening letter to
the Premier, Mr R Hamer.

Judge Martin assisted his Tipstaff and two prison
officers to tackle Read and, assisted by police, overpowered him. He was taken into custody and held in the
County Court cells.

They have requested that Read be transferred to H
Division as soon as the legal formalities are completed.

N L Doyle.

FILE NOTE
74/4480

26 April 1976

Interviewed in G Division. He is to appear in court (St Kilda) tomorrow 27/4/78 on charges of assault. He does not know when his Supreme Court case is on.

Mark is in a quite jocular state, asking how much do I think he'll get for his offences. Explains he doesn't think he's done anything really serious. With regard to the assault, he claims that the man he attacked was a hoon and he deserved what he got, the police stood and watched him and agreed it was deserved. Mark feels he has done the community a service. Asked about his attempted abduction of Judge Martin, had he thought he could pull it off? Says yes, Loughnan had said that terrorism always worked: 'they shit themselves'. Mark very surprised when there was retaliation; now feels he went about it the wrong way, he should have pulled the gun and ordered everyone not to move before approaching Judge Martin. He only intended to hold him for an hour so that Loughnan could be given a car and a gun. Says always listens to Loughnan, although is now considering that perhaps his advice is not too good. They had planned an escape from hospital and Loughnan gave him a handful of 'hardware' to swallow. Much to Read's disgust he did not see a doctor till three days later.

Asked about his ears: says decided he would do a 'Van Gogh' needed to draw attention to himself drastically as wrists didn't attract enough attention, 'everybody does that.' States that he got Kevin Taylor to cut them off. He started to saw at one and then Mark said, 'Don't saw, slash it off', which Taylor did. He then did the same to the other one and then vomited. Mark under the impression that you didn't lose much blood when you cut ears off and was surprised to lose five pints. Also thought it could be sewn back on again quite easily. Thought he might be declared insane after this but when advised could end up a Governor's Pleasure decided 'he couldn't win'.

Mark seems to want assurances that his offences are not really serious, whilst inviting the prison officer to assure that they really are extremely audacious and daring. No comments were elicited. The relation of these offences by Read were done in a light-hearted and humorous fashion, which made it extremely difficult to keep a straight face. However there is little doubt that Mark's impetuosity is extremely dangerous. I do not think that anyone would disagree that this lad is a true-blue psychopath. An earlier diagnosis of autism is interesting, as is father's presentation.

28 November 1978

The Superintendent,
H. M. Prison, Pentridge.
Self inflicted injury on prisoner
Mark Read, H Division.

Sir,

On Monday 27 November 1978 it was reported to me at 1.10pm by acting chief prison officer Hildebrand that H Division prisoner, Mark Read, had inflicted three slashes to his right cheek with a razor blade.

He had been talking to Jimmy Loughnan in No. 2

yard who told him that the only way to get out of 'H' was to slash up. Read said that he had slashed his cheek three times thinking he would spend Christmas in hospital.

Read was returned to No. 2 yard after he made his statement. He immediately went up to Loughnan and another prisoner and said: 'I am taking no more notice of you two, I slashed my face for nothing.'

Over the same incident, another prison officer reported Read said, 'Sir, I seem to have cut my face, could you get a medic, with a couple of asprins and a couple of bandaids.' I asked him if he felt the wounds were serious and he replied, 'No Sir, a couple of bandaids will do.'

PRISONER APPLICATION FOR RECLASSIFICATION

Dear Sir,

I would rather not linger too long in this division or in Pentridge. I would like to get to a nice, easy-going country jail and out of the way altogether. So as soon as you think I've proved that I can live peacefully with my fellow man or whenever you think you can talk the Director General into it, I'd like to get the hell out of here.

I am very grateful for being given the chance to get out of Jika and to come to J of all places.

I guess I feel like a man who has to keep changing trains to get the last one home. H was the start, G was a stop over, then back to H, then on to Jika Jika, now J Division.

I guess I won't really be able to relax in my mind until I am on the last train home when I can say, right this is it, no more questioning and wondering. I guess after six years of maximum security divisions and my last sentence was mostly in H Division, with a bit of D and B Division tossed in, the J Division set is real fantasy land.

Since I have been in Pentridge, I have had a bad run with personal relationships, they come and go. If I get to a country jail and get a local guy who's doing time to put me on to a local girl and get visits every week. Jika messed up my last relationship and if I bother to try and get a new friend, she will only drop off when I get sent away. So I've got a few reasons for wanting to get to a nice country jail and do it easy.

Thank you very much.

PS: Beechworth sounds nice. Geelong is a dirty old hole. Thank you very much.

Mark Brandon Read,

model prisoner and totally reformed.

ASSAULT BY STABBING OF PRISONER

Wednesday, 7 January 1981

Prisoners Tsakmakis and Mark Read were alone in day room one of unit two, Jika Jika, about 10.30am on 7 January 1981, when apparently Tsakmakis was discussing a prisoner in B Division with Read. The man is an enemy of both prisoners. Read requested to cease the conversation and after further comments Read lost his temper and a scuffle ensued. Tsakmakis requested to be let out of the day room, however Read followed him with a pair of tailoring shears. Read cornered him in the unit shower room and stabbed him several times with the shears.

G.F. MYERS
Superintendent.

Dear Classo Board.

I would very much like to go back into the same yard as Alex Tsakmakis, I like him and I get on very well with him. Unfortunately, I took a turn for the worse today, and very nearly made a fatal mistake. I am very sorry for this, the wrong thing was said at the wrong time. I was worried and upset about another matter and Alex said something to me that upset me for a moment.

I was in the wrong, by taking the action that I did. I'm sorry if you do not want to put me back into the yard with Alex, I will understand your action, but neverthless I have no plans to harm Alex and I do not believe he has a plan to harm me in any way. I know that you all believe me to be a smiling mad man, and I have done nothing to prove you wrong. If you do not put me and Alex back together again, then what? Problems, problems, problems. I feel that I should give some form of explanation re: my actions towards Alex Tsakmakis.

I was in a very sad mood after a visit with my father. I had been let down badly by a newspaper man who had for the last year claimed to be writing a book about me. My father plans to go down to Tassie in four years time, leaving me here on my own.

I know that I will rot in this Division forever and a day. I am bored stiff and I am slowly going out of my mind in this place. I'm doing a 17½ year sentence over a man who betrayed me and, from my point of view, my life is hopeless, and I have nothing in the world to lose.

Alex made a smart comment at the wrong time that just made my mind snap. Alex did not mean to say anything wrong, he did not understand my state of mind. It was not his fault. Another thing, you have never given me any hope since I started this sentence, you dump me in H Division and now Jika without a shred of hope. I don't know if I'm ever going to see a country jail, I don't know if I'm going to get parole or not. I would like to do weightlifting, that's why I want to go back to G Division, or a country jail. I would not escape. You dump me here with nothing to do, and then you cannot understand when I go off my head once in a while. I have never harmed a prison officer because I have always felt that if I could be trusted in that way then that at least would be one small favour. Anyway, I know that nothing I say or do will change your minds about me.

Once again, I would like to go back with Alex Tsakmakis. Question. Why is it that you always put me in spots where I have nothing to lose and then you wonder why I crack up now and again? Why don't you try doing me a good turn instead of a bad turn and you would find out that I would never let you down.

Take G Division, for example. To my way of thinking this jail has done Mark Brandon Read no bloody favours. You have offered me no hope at all. It has been one line of labour yards, observation cells, H Division and Jika Jika, from the word go. When I arrived in Pentridge in

1975 I have been placed in spots where trouble would have to erupt.

If I was a paranoid person, I could easily believe that you have placed me in spots where you knew that sooner or later blood would flow and my body, or someone else's, would be carried out in a bag.

The only division I have ever been in that did not upset me was G Division. I got on very well there, but they got paranoid of me, or did they? I still don't know why I was moved and if there is anyone in Pentridge who really needs to be in G Division it is me.

Anyway, if I can't go back with Alex, could you please find some harmless, inoffensive person for me to go in with. Someone I know will not attack me. I would not harm a harmless person.

1984

Read is currently located in J Division and is serving a sentence of 14/11 years.

He has applied for a transfer to Geelong and this has been recommended by the Review and Assessment. The governor of Geelong is prepared to accept the prisoner and Mr Snook has given his support to the transfer. Mr Hecker stated that the prisoner should be transferred because he has taken the initiative and done what was required of him.

CLASSIFICATION ANNUAL REVIEW

Chief or senior prison officer's report:
No problem since he arrived at Geelong.

Welfare Officer's Report:
Mark has been at Geelong for several months and appears to have settled in satisfactorily. He mixes little with other inmates with the exception of a select few. He makes few requests and no demands.

Governor's report:
Read has not encountered any problems since his arrival at Geelong. He is a deep-thinking type who keeps very much to himself. He needs supervision because of his record and his heavy medication. Recommended that he remain at Geelong. Review in December 1984.

MEMORANDUM

21 December 1984

Prisoner Read has been at Geelong since March 1984. His conduct on the surface has been excellent. Lately he has been receiving what he calls 'gifts from other prisoners'. He has never purchased a canteen, but is never without canteen items.

TRANSFER DETAILS

21 December

Prisoner's name: READ, Mark Brandon.
Transfer details: To H Division.
Reason for transfer: Suspected of standing over other prisoners for personal gain.

28 December 1984

Dear Mr Johnson;

How are you sir? Well, it is me again, back in Pentridge H Division.

As we both know sir, I gave you my word that I would not, to put it bluntly, 'shit in your face', if given the chance to go away, and it was with this in mind that I went out of my way to do the right thing in Geelong. In fact I really went out of my way, becoming an almost changed man, and not allowing pride to get in the way of common sense, or my promise to you.

I have not been told why I'm here in H Division. Geelong wouldn't or couldn't tell me. I was unable to see the Governor but the chief told me 'it was nothing to do' with Geelong or any suspected wrong doing on my part down there.

I just don't want you thinking that my coming back to Pen has meant that I've broken my word to you as I pride myself on, once giving my word, keeping it as I don't run around making two bob promises all around the jail.

To be honest, I don't want you getting dirty on me when I know, in my own mind, I'm guilty of nothing apart from possibly being Mark Brandon Read, victim of 1,000 whispers. I just want it understood, between us, that my word has not been broken. Not one drop of Geelong blood was ever spilt. I raised my hand to no one down there, much to my disgust, I might add.

Since I've been back I've heard whispers that I was moved as a result of the Loughnan escape or poison pen letters under the doors and in the mail box or crying mothers on the phone asking that their sons be protected from the dreaded beast with no ears.

I am no saint, but I'm not a liar either. My downfall is that because I am what I am and who I am, I either am outright guilty or giving the appearance of being guilty.

Not one person has bothered to confront me face to face on any matter of wrongdoing or suspected wrongdoing, so I hope this in not head office paranoia – no offence meant. I've come too far now Mr J to go through a replay of the late '70s. I couldn't face it all again.

I'm tired, I've had enough. I've got two, two and a half years to go. I haven't crossed you, or the Governor of Geelong. I've done the right thing. I've tried as hard as I can. Please, whatever it is that is going on, can we sort it out? I've just had enough, I just want to do my time and get out.

All the best,

Mark Brandon Read.

RELEASED FROM JAIL IN NOVEMBER 1986

File Notes.

November 25, 1986

Mark Read

Read attended this evening at 6pm as required. He instantly recognised a large potential problem in another pre-release. Apparently Read was involved in an incident in prison in 1975 where the other man was hit with a baseball bat, and there has been ill-feeling between the groups ever since.

Both parties reacted significantly this evening, which makes the writer feel there is probably mostly truth in the allegations. It is our intention to have Read report to the centre at 1pm this Thursday, 27 November to 'do' his three hours.

At this time a future possible placement will be discussed, as a psychiatric referral (which has been requested by Read).

Read left the centre (with permission) at 7.30pm.

Gerry O'Donnell.

Read recalls:

IN November 1986 I was released from Bendigo Prison and ordered to report to the pre-release attendance centre in Carlton, it was situated near Lygon Street, in fact, it could be seen clearly from the Bowling Green Hotel, where Dennis Allen sometimes drank while waiting for his mother, who also had to report there. When I went in, she saw me and ran screaming into the office ranting and raving about how I had bashed her young son Dennis over his pinhead with a baseball bat. Actually, I did him a favour, because he had a head which needed regular panel beating.

There was some other non-event, two-bob gangster there as well, who joined in on the baseball bat story, and complained that I'd hit him with a baseball bat as well. Who did these characters think I was, Babe Ruth?

I told the people in charge that this was total nonsense.

I had in fact hit Allen over the head nine times with a large rolling pin. I thought he 'kneaded' it, ha ha.

As for the other numbskull, I hit him with a mop bucket, there was never a baseball bat in sight. Nevertheless, they refused to accept me at the attendance centre. All in all, they sent me to two more attendance centres, but it was the same old story. Every time I would walk in, some crim would run to the office and sob out a story about how I had allegedly flogged him inside. In the end, they told me not to come in and just to check in via the phone. The Parole Board ended up sending me to Tasmania as it was easier for all concerned.

My popularity or lack of it in criminal circles was always a problem for the Parole Board. I was as popular as a hand grenade in a wedding cake. Bugger it, popularity has never been the aim of the game in my mind.

File note

1 December 1986

From Mark Read.

He claims to have spoken to a member of the police force who stated that he should watch his back and there are people who will hunt you down no matter what. Mark is concerned that he will be shot while at the attendance centre. He stated he would prefer to be back in prison.

Mark added that he does have a lot of enemies – people who 'use speed and get paranoid' and that he does not think he is paranoid himself. He is worried that if these people find out he is attending the Glenhuntly Community Corrections Centre, they will come to this office and put a 'bullet in my back'. He does not want to keep moving from one corrections centre to another throughout his pre-release.

File note

12 December 1986

Jocelyn Pitt, assistant regional manager, Inner Urban, phoned regarding a phone call they had received from the police which indicated Read may be in danger.

Apparently he is involved with some feuding families in the inner urban region and there could be people who are interested in doing harm to him. The police indicated there was nothing they could do, but Jocelyn suggests that it may be appropriate to allow some flexibility for Read's reporting, so that he cannot be readily tracked down by other people, and we should afford him whatever protection we can.

Community based corrections

26 November 1986

ADULT PROBATION. 4. Breached. 4.
ADULT PAROLE. 4. Breached. 4.

16 December 1986

Probation and Parole Office,
111–113 Cameron Street,
Launceston. Tas. 7250.

Attention: Mr Beckett.
RE: Mark Brandon READ.
Born: 17-11-54.
Pre-release then parole.
On the 15-12-86 Read was given permission to leave Victoria to reside in Tasmania by the Adult Parole Board of Victoria.

He is leaving Victoria on the 15-12-86 and will live with his father in Ravenswood, Launceston.

I am making a request of your office to supervise Read during his pre-release then his parole period.

Read was released from Bendigo Prison on 24-11-86, his permit will then run until the 28-10-87, he will then be released on a parole order. This office will send you a parole order for him to sign towards the end of his pre-release permit.

Although Read has an extensive criminal history I do not believe he will cause you any concern. Read left Victoria because an element of the Melbourne Criminal Society is looking for him and he would rather not be found.

I have told Read not to contact your office until he received a letter from you. He has also been asked to keep in contact with the writer. Please find enclosed a copy of his pre-release permit. Could you please send me quarterly reports on Read's progress.

If I can be of any further assistance please contact me at the above address,

Yours faithfully.
Jim Jeffery,
Acting assistant regional manager,
Northcote Community Corrections.

Mark Brandon Read
Unit 11/ No 1, Blyth St
Ravenswood, Launceston
Tasmania 7250.

Hello Mr Jeffery,

It is I, Chopper, alive and well in the rural splendor of Tasmania. I'm on the dole, I've got a bank account with the Launceston Bank of Savings.

Dad introduced me to the police within half an hour of me getting off the plane. My sins in the mainland mean nothing in their eyes down here.

If anyone farts in my general direction, from a distance of 300 yards, they are in bother. Ha ha.

Thank you for your help and understanding in this matter. Maybe one day, I may be able to do you a kindness. What more can I say apart from take care and thank you once again.

Regards,

Mark Brandon Read.

After Read was released from jail on 24 November 1986, he claimed to be finished with crime and living quietly in Tasmania. But retirement was not for him; he secretly returned to Melbourne for hit run raids on drug dealers. In the early hours of 12 June 1987, Read went to the Bojangles Nightclub and shot dead 'Sammy the Turk, Siam Ozerkam. Read was charged with murder. But while he never denied shooting Ozerkam in the left eye with a shotgun at point-blank range, he claimed it was self-defence. In the end, to his surprise, the jury believed him and he was acquitted of murder.

Mark Brandon Read
H Div
PO Box 114
Coburg, Vic, 3058.

Dear Mr Jeffery,

I received a couple of notices from the parole people — orders for the cancellation of my pre-release permit. Is this a normal state of affairs? And how does this leave me?

Should I be granted bail or found not guilty at court, what the hell did you tell them in your report?

If I am granted bail can anything be done? A bribe is not totally out of the question. If I am found not guilty, where do I stand? I hope this does not mean my parole is cancelled.

My God, all this fuss over a wog. Murder should be a five bob fine. Murder is too strong a word in this instance. I guess one could explain it away as Anglo-Turkish relations gone wrong.

I'd rather be tried by 12 than carried by six. Surely the Parole Board can wait to flex their biceps till after I'm found guilty, and that hasn't happened yet. God is a Mason and a white man and he will protect me.

Let me know what's going on.

Thank you,

Mark Brandon Read Esq.

July 29, 1987

To Mr Mark Read,
H Division, Pentridge

Dear Mark,

In answer to your question regarding pre-release.

It is the practice of the Parole Board to cancel a pre-release permit when the conditions of the permit cannot be complied with. In your case you are in custody and cannot comply with the conditions. Should you be given bail the board does have the power to then release you on pre-release, but looking at the charge you are now facing I do not believe the board would release you.

Should you be found not guilty or the matter is withdrawn by the Crown, the board would look at your case. The board has the power to keep you inside or release you, that is up to the board. I would think that the chances of being released are good, but that is only my opinion.

Mark, a bribe is totally out of the question. I am not prepared to comment on your comments about Anglo-

Turkish relations, or if God is a Mason.
Yours Sincerely,

Jim Jeffery,
Acting Assistant Regional Manager,
Northcote Community Corrections Centre.

November 5, 1987

Mark Brandon Read
H Div
PO Box 114
Coburg Vic, 3058

Dear Mr Jeffery,

Dear Sir, It is I, Mark Brandon Read Esq, my case is under investigation by the Victorian police Internal Security Unit, and the National Crime Authority.

By the way, please excuse my poor spelling and bad grammar, I'm in on a murder charge and not company fraud. I've asked the ISU if I could be placed or released into their custody. They said they could not, but they told me to apply for bail. I've asked the NCA if I could be released into their custody until my court case. I have not heard an answer from them on this yet.

I have no fear on my so-called murder charge. I have given the ISU enough evidence in relation to police corruption to sink a battleship, and I haven't begun to give the NCA a real 'earful' yet. In the beginning my bail was refused. All this and more is in 43 Stat. Decks. (sic) being looked into by the ISU and NCA.

The point is, Mr Jeffery, if the ISU or NCA recommend me for bail, would that bugger up re: my pre-release and parole. Would it be a stumbling block? Wild horses couldn't keep me from my upcoming court case. I've got enough on the scallywags to start a Royal Commission and I intend to dump a ton of police dirty washing before the court. I am unsure of the power of the NCA, but if they agree to release me into their custody, would the parole situation be a snag?

If they strongly recommend bail, could I be bailed considering my pre-release and parole situation. The efforts on my part re: seeing the NCA and release into their custody and bail won't be a going concern for a month or two yet. I'd just like to know where I stand with the parole and pre-release situation. Hence my letter to your good self as I find it hard to conduct my legal battles from behind bluestone walls.

Please check this out for me.

Thank you – all the best.

Chopper.

MEMORANDUM

To: Mr R Wise, supervisor.
From: Chairperson, H Division Review and Assessment
Committee.

Date: **6 December 1990**

Re: Placement options for prisoner (3403)
Mark Brandon READ.

Read was received into Office of Corrections custody on
this occasion on 2 July 1987, charged with the murder of
Siam Ozerkam. The killing having occurred outside
Bojangles Nightclub on 12 June 1987.

Upon reception Read was placed in H Division, where
he remained until his move to K Division, again being
returned to H Division (30 October 1987) after the
closure of Jika Jika. Has remained in H Division since
that time.

The reason for Read's continued retention in a high
security environment is that it has been considered that if
he were to be placed anywhere else, either he would be
the victim of violence or he would use force against
others, this primarily as a result of him offending against
the criminal world when last at freedom, but also, due to
his activities during this sentence.

When received in July, 1989, Read submitted a
request for protection which read: 'protection required
from anyone who looks sideways at me – if prisoner
Read is provided with a knife, protection would not be
required ... prisoner Read is unpopular within criminal

circles as prisoner Read stands for truth, justice and the Australian way.'

Read readily admits that when last at freedom (from 26 November 1986 – 2 July 1987) and subject to a pre-release permit and while allegedly living in Tasmania, he made frequent trips to Melbourne (he says two weeks out of every month) during which he involved himself in standing over others in the criminal world. He has even alleged that he engaged in these activities on behalf of some members of the police force and that when he killed Ozerkam he was wearing a bullet-proof vest provided by the armed robbery squad and he was driven from the scene by police officers from the Bureau of Criminal Intelligence (BCI). Read described his acquittal on the murder of Ozerkam as a 'miracle'.

Read is currently serving five years maximum – two years six months minimum for intention to cause injury, which relates to the shooting and wounding of Chris Liapis, and arson and reckless conduct, which relates to the shooting of and the burning down of the home of a drug dealer's mother. Again Read claims he was acting as a police enforcer in those matters and has made this claim in an affidavit to the Homicide Squad and at the murder trial and at the trial relating to the Liapis shooting and the burning of the house.

Read would have to be considered one of this state's most notorious prisoners, not because of the management concerns he currently causes but because of his involvement in a series of bizarre incidents, and his bald acceptance of a life of violence and crime.

As you are aware, in the late 1970s Read involved himself in some bizarre mutilations. First, having both ears cut off, later saying he thought (mistakenly) that the operation would be bloodless and that his ears could be reattached, and that, while not painful, the amputation made a 'very nasty noise'. Second, by attempting to blind himself with a lit cigarette and third, by slashing his face.

Similarly, his offences have been out of the ordinary. He has attempted to kidnap a County Court judge, only to be overpowered in the court by the Tipstaff and prison officers. The motive for the incident being that he wanted the release of his friend, James Loughnan from J ward. He has been involved in stabbing other very influential prisoners like Alex Tsakmakis (now deceased) and he has been involved in factional fights which have led to him falling out with prisoners.

With that background (not aided by the nickname of Chopper), Read regularly features in the media and does not shy away from such attention. In February 1990, a series of articles ('The Chopper Read File') were published in *The Sun* newspaper. Read was described as a 'Bounty Hunter', who 'calmly stalks criminals, killing, shooting and bashing as he sees fit'. Also in February 1990 it was reported that 'Police and Office of Corrections have confirmed the renewal of a contract allegedly of $50,000 on Read's life, that money being supplied by a drug syndicate'. It was also reported that Judge Dyett in the County Court in December 1989, was satisfied that a contract had been taken out on Read's life as a result of him being known as a police informer.

Most recently, of course, Read has been mentioned in the media coverage of allegations that a Ku Klux Klan cell existed in H Division (himself being photographed wearing a Ku Klux Klan type hood). As a result of an

Administrative Appeals Tribunal into whether investigation documents relating to the Ku Klux Klan activities should be released to the Prison Reform Group, Read has written to newspapers saying that there was no Ku Klux Klan in H Division, and by having the matter aired in public for an extended period the potential existed to actually create a Klan where none previously existed. His views on the matter were again reported to the press.

Against that background the H Division Review and Assessment considered Read's case on 5 December 1990, at which time the committee exhausted all possible placement options.

For his part, Read expressed his desire to remain in H Division until his release for two reasons. First, he has concerns for his own safety. When previously discussing a Loddon placement he claimed to fear some of the 'young, up and coming' prisoners who may well seek to 'sneak go' him as he believes he would be an important 'scalp' to have on their belt. Second, his girlfriend lives in Collingwood and finds visiting Coburg convenient; he says because her car is in such poor repair that it will only just make the Coburg trip.

Placement of Read at one of the protection prisons (Beechworth or Sale) is, the Committee believes, out of the question given Read's history of violence.

Bearing all the above in mind, the Committee recommends that Read remain in H Division as no other placement options exist for him at this time. As usual Read is extremely happy with this arrangement. Having recommended that Read remain in H Division, one needs to address the issue of preparation for Read's release.

As is known, not only did Read regress, he was

received back into Office of Corrections custody on a Capital charge, close supervision proved impossible given his protection concerns, his continuing offending in the criminal community and his move to Tasmania (albeit on a part-time basis).

K Anderson
Chairperson
H Division Review and Assessment Committee

Review and Assessment Committee
Annual Review.
Name: READ, Mark.

Review

20 December 1989

Read was sentenced on 19/12/89 to five years – two years six months minimum.

As usual 'happy go lucky' presentation. 'How's that, two shootings and I got 20 months, not bad.' Says he wishes to remain in H Division. As usual making jokes and comments about the criminal justice system.

5 June 1991

Prisoner to be seen as a review. Was seen by the Adult Parole Board 31/05/91, who have decided that they will not release Read at this time. His case will be reviewed in late '91. All agree review in three months.

Prisoner seen. Says the Parole Board have indicated he

will be released late '91, however are keen to keep the date quiet. He also said please keep the date quiet. Says he will go to Tasmania upon release and just let anyone come after him there. The 'Carlton Crew' (see media) were behind the incident which led to Ozerkam being killed.

That he has sent out material to Carlton Crew showing just what type of persons they all are. That reports that a $30,000 contract taken out on his life are real, however, it would-be hard to collect in Tasmania because anyone trying to fill the contract would be on his home turf and he had many friends/associates in Tasmania.

Says he has prepared for release, has all his money etc.

Remain in H, review on 4 September 1991.

He is only waiting to go home.

As usual, most entertaining, however, underlying all his stories is the constant threat of extreme violence.

31 July 1991

Name: READ, Mark

Prisoner seen as annual review. Has apparently been given indications by the Parole Board that he will be granted parole in November, 1991, with little forewarning. Happy in H Division and not interested in Loddon, Morwell River release preparation (he already has his identification papers, etc.) and his only concern is that he gets a cash advance so that he doesn't have to cash an Office of Corrections cheque to buy tickets to Tasmania, etc. As always, in good humour and speaking totally unrealistically, one expects, of retiring to the good life and not coming back to Victoria.

CHAPTER 19

A SLOW LEARNER NEVER FORGETS

'I HELD UP MY HAND AND SAID,
"GIVE US A HAND". HE LAUGHED AND SAID,
"HELLO, CHOP CHOP, I'LL GIVE YOU A
HAND ALL RIGHT". THEN HE KICKED
ME IN THE FACE'

ONE of the worst beatings I ever received was at the tender age of 12 years. A team of us from Thomastown, aged between 12 and 16, hopped on a train and headed for Collingwood. There was between 15 and 20 of us. It was a long time ago but I can still remember about a dozen of the kids in the gang.

We had a plan, and that was to head to Collingwood and attack the local bucks. I said we had a plan. I didn't say it was a good plan. The idea was that no one would be stupid enough to go into the Collingwood boys' home turf and attack them there, so the theory was we would have the element of surprise and could launch an ambush. It was the sort of brain-dead plan that General Custer once hatched, and it didn't do him any good either.

I went along with the boys in this hare-brained venture with a feeling of impending doom. I knew enough about Collingwood to know that regardless of numbers, or surprise or ambush, you just didn't go up there for a fight and come away with a victory.

The bunch we planned to attack were about our own ages. I knew them quite well as my father had a number of relatives in the area from Northcote to Richmond, and the gangs included quite a number of my cousins.

I was ill at ease about the whole nitwit idea, but I went along for the ride. We got off at Victoria Park railway station and proceeded towards the Collingwood Football Ground, where we knew the local lads used to hang out. You don't have to be told … we were ambushed straight away by what seemed to be a million Collingwood kids.

I fought bravely for all of two seconds, until I got smashed to the ground by a kid smaller than myself. I got up and got knocked down, this time by a kid about half my size. I got up again, this time to be downed by a girl swinging a bike pump.

I was woozy, bleeding and out of my depth. I looked up to see a cousin of mine, looking down on me with a big grin. Thank goodness, I thought, a friendly face in a sea of hostility.

I held up my hand and said, 'Give us a hand'. He laughed and said, 'Hello, Chop Chop, I'll give you a hand all right'. Then he kicked me in the face. I said we were related. I didn't say we were close.

I was dragged to my feet and blindfolded with a hanky which must have belonged to a kid with a bad cold. My hands were tied with what I later found was sticky tape and I was taken prisoner.

Youthful games, you may think. What would they make me do? Eat a tadpole? Eat dirt? No, this was Collingwood and I had been part of a crew that had tried to take them on. I knew that even though we were kids, my punishment would not be kid's stuff.

I was marched off by a gang of the Collingwood kids, my assorted cousins among them. The rest of the Thomastown kids were being punched into 10 shades of shit, with a few having escaped at 100 miles per hour. So much for the heavy thinking which had gone into this great battle plan. Half the team were bleeding buckets and the rest had run like French poodles. But I didn't get the chance to slink off into the distance, because I was the prize prisoner.

They took me to a small gravel car park near the footy club.

One of the kids was told to rush home and grab a pillow case. We all stood there, waiting. I tried to talk my way out of the problem but I got a smack in the mouth for my trouble.

The kid returned with a pillow case. They put it over my head and tied it around my neck with an old bootlace. Another bootlace was tied around my wrists, behind my back. I was helpless – and then it started. I was punched in the head repeatedly. I tried to run to the left, and got fists from that direction. I tried to run to the right and got the same again. My face felt warm and wet. I could taste my own blood in my mouth. All I could see were the star-like flashes of light you get behind your closed eyelids and inside your head when you are punched in the darkness.

I was blinded and being beaten for what seemed like ages. I fell to the ground and tried to hide my face in the gravel, but they kicked me in the head. My face was hot and very wet with blood. Then the beating stopped and the pillow case was ripped off my head, leaving the hanky, now red with blood, around my face. I could see a bit, but my eyes were nearly closed. My face was a bashed-in mess of blood.

My hands were cut free and the gang simply walked away. I lay in the car park. I was crying, and the hot salty tears stung my eyes and the cuts on my face. I got up and limped off. The beating had come from kids aged 10 to 15. It had been brutal. Why had I been sorted out for special attention?

The answer was simple. I had cousins in Collingwood, and I had dared come up to Collingwood with a crew from Thomastown to fight my own relatives. I was a traitor and I deserved special attention. I felt like a traitor. And the experience of being beaten, punched and kicked in the head while blindfolded is something I will never forget.

I got back to the Victoria Park railway station and got the train back to Thomastown. My face was swollen and my eyes nearly closed up. I felt like mincemeat. But it taught me a good lesson about violence, pain and bloodshed. It also taught me never to attack anyone on their playing field, or in their own back yard.

It didn't matter whether it was Thomastown kids going to Collingwood or Uncle Sam going to Vietnam, no one comes out with a victory fighting anyone in their own back yard. You might win a few sneak attacks but mostly you'll get done like a dinner. People fight harder to protect what they believe is theirs ...

Seven years later I ended up in St Vincent's Hospital for a few running repairs after me and another bloke had a punch-on in a city pub. We both fell through a glass door inside the pub. I had to get some glass taken out of my head and a bit of general stitching. The other bloke had to go into surgery after getting a sliver of glass about two inches long wedged in his right eyeball.

It's not like the movies, when you fall through a glass door. It can really cuts the guts out of you. It's a good way to stop a fight. We both stopped immediately. They managed to save his eyeball, and pulled the glass out of me, so all was well. But at the hospital, I was left sitting in the casualty area for about 45 minutes with blood seeping out of my head at a steady dribble, while they attended to more serious cases.

A young nurse named Colleen spoke to me and asked if my name was Mark Read. I said yes and then she said, 'Chop Chop.' I said, 'No, Chopper.'

She then asked if I remembered her and I didn't. She simply said, 'Victoria Park Railway Station, 1967.' She then explained that she was the girl who had smashed me over the head with a bike pump and gave me a few to go on with in the car park. She had kicked me in the face while I was lying in the gravel. Hardly the training for a future nurse, I would have thought.

We had a good laugh about it. She was a tall girl, about five foot eleven and as skinny as a bean pole. She had a nice face, but swore like a drunken sailor. I took a dislike to the skinny cow right away, but I smiled and laughed along with her.

I invited her to go out with me and to my surprise she said yes and I picked her up from work two weeks later. We had a good time together, but I was really pumping the grog into her. She was blind drunk, and falling about all over the place, smashed off her face.

If there is one thing I can do, it is drink and still think and stand up. We ended up in a pub in Kensington. I have no idea how we managed that but she ended up passing out in the back of a taxi on the way to Port Melbourne. I didn't know what to do with her, so I got out of the cab and heaved her over my shoulder.

I had planned to get her drunk and have my wicked way with her. But once they pass out, it's against the rules, so I was left walking along with her over my shoulder. I had no idea what to do with this sleeping, drunken, Collingwood, bike pump-swinging nurse.

I don't know how long it took me to get there, but eventually I ended up on the banks of Albert Park Lake. I then did the natural and gentlemanly thing.

I threw her in the drink.

Who said chivalry is dead? She was drunk and fully clothed. Splash. In she went and sunk like a rock, then up she came with a gasp and a cough, mixed with a scream, then down she went again, thrashing around like a drowning cat. The water was only about three feet deep. I reached down, grabbed her and yanked her out.

If she had just stood up she could have got out herself. I said to her, 'You stupid cow, you fell in the water'. She was in tears, sobbing and spluttering her thanks to me for saving her. Ha ha.

She wanted to be taken home, so we went back to her flat and after a hot shower and a couple of drinks, Bike Pump Colleen repaid me very nicely for saving her life.

Now I know the secret of being a ladies man. Get them pissed and toss them in the drink.

When my ears came off in February 1978, I went to St Vincent's, and Colleen was still on the scene. I was being guarded by three screws and she was on the night shift. She came to visit me and sat on my bed, holding my hands. She turned to the screws and said, 'Do you know this wonderful man saved me from drowning?'

Having just had my ears sewn back on, I was not in good humour, but hearing her say that, I burst out laughing. She joined in and so did the screws, but I was the only one who knew the real joke.

Ah, you wouldn't be dead for quids. Not with the present interest rates, any rate.

WHILE the pillow case over the head was a horrific thrashing, it wasn't the only top serve I'd been given as a kid. I got pulled into several crazy plots and plans, and got left posted, resulting in blood hitting the footpath.

In the 1960s there were no weird groups and cults in Melbourne. No punks, skunks, Nazis and brain-dead, glue-sniffing creeps out to break into your house to steal the video, shit on your carpet and rape the cat. In those days there were only three gangs, or styles, for the type of youths looking for a bit of action. There were the Mods, with their long hair; the Rockers, with the slicked-back, oiled-up hair, all looking like bad Elvis impersonators, and the Sharpies, with their semi-crew cuts and chisel-toe shoes. The Thomastown boys were all Sharpies, although, now and again, I'd flirt with the Rocker look (I had ears then). But I would always end up back at the barber's for my old square back, semi-crew cut.

One of the old streetfighting tricks of the day was to get a little kid to taunt and tease another gang with foul abuse about 100 feet away, and when the larger gang jumped in to teach the shrimp some manners, they would be led into a trap. They would chase the little kid around a corner or up a lane way to find that a larger gang was lying in wait for them. It was a classic ambush. I was often asked to be the bait for such ambush attacks.

The Thomastown and Keon Park Sharpies, ages ranging from 15 to 19, would jump on the train and do battle with the Rockers from West Richmond, Preston or Reservoir. A few stupid kids like myself were always conned into coming along. On one occasion in December 1967, when I was 13, about 20 or 30 of the local boys were waiting at the West Richmond railway station for the big battle. Me and another little idiot were ordered to smash a window of a pool room, about two blocks away. We knew it was the local haunt of the Rockers and the plan was to lure them back for the ambush.

We did what we were told. The other kid took one look at the 20 or so tough-looking Rockers who spilled out of the joint and beat a hasty, and wise, retreat. I was on the other side of the road and started to yell out to the gang. I threw out a few choice insults and then started to run like hell. But nothing happened, they just wouldn't follow.

I mean they weren't silly, and the trick of sending in a kid to act as the lure was not exactly a secret. The Richmond and Collingwood boys invented it, for goodness sake. But I was too thick to know that so I kept a constant stream of abuse flowing their way, at a safe distance of around 50 to 60 yards. As I got braver, the abuse became stronger, I even suggested that I had been involved in some form of sexual dalliance with their respective mothers. Back in the '60s, any reference to mothers of a slanderous nature would not be tolerated, and could not be ignored. I kept it up. 'Come on you weak dogs, I'll fight the lot of you,' I said. I was getting braver by the minute as they still showed no signs of moving in my direction.

I then singled out one of their crew for special attention, a big bloke, about 19, with blond hair and a head like a pineapple. They were calling to him to forget it. 'Come on Normie, it's a stooge set-up,' they said. And they were right, but I could see that Normie was getting agitated so I drop a real winner. I suggested to Old Normie that his sister may have been having an affair with an Italian chappie. The fact that I didn't know Normie from a bar of soap, or whether he even had a sister, had little to do with it, but it worked immediately.

Normie spat the dummy and was off after me with three or four of his crew in tow. 'Ha, ha,' I thought as I ran back at top speed back to the railway station, 'are these wombats going to get it.'

They were hot on my heels, about 20 feet behind and closing fast. I pelted down a narrow street and through the station gates with Normie and his mates in hot pursuit as I got on to the platform.

It was empty.

The Thomastown and Keon Park boys had all gone for a drink after the other kid had run back and said they wouldn't take the bait. Well, that was what I got told later.

As I hit the empty railway station, my heart sank. Normie and his mates grabbed me, and did I get a flogging. I was kicked to ribbons. But Normie pulled up and said, 'Leave it, the poor bugger has been left posted'. It was obvious it was a stooge set-up, and Normie and his crew were almost as shocked as I was that I had led them into an empty ambush.

But still, my remarks about their mothers and Normie's sister, including the very unwise crack about her involvement with members of the animal kingdom, had to be punished. Comments like that should be left to Australian cricketers to make in good-natured sledging.

I swore then that I would not act as bait for an ambush in a street battle ever again. Which I didn't – until I got talked into doing the same thing against a gang of long-haired Mods from Reservoir another time. Maybe they were right at school when they said I was a slow learner.

My crew was waiting in a car park near the Reservoir police

station. It was a quiet Sunday afternoon, and believe it or not, the cop shop was shut, either that or the police had been out on the tear on Saturday and were sleeping it off while on duty.

It was my job to tease and taunt this gang of long-haired Mods who hung around the Reservoir railway station. I started with the tried and true line of witticisms, which involved their mothers, sisters and girlfriends having unsavoury relationships with German Shepherd dogs and off-duty policeman, but it was to no avail.

These long hairs would not take the bait. It was only when I began tossing stones at them, one of which hit one of their lady friends right in the face, that we got some action. It certainly broke the ice. They all ran off after me and I headed off to the car park as was arranged. When I got there, you guessed it, I was left high and dry again.

This time it was a practical joke. My so-called mates had cleared off in the name of good humour. I could not see the joke at the time. I was pissing blood for a week because of the kicking I got. Is it any wonder I grew up so bitter and twisted? Even today I still believe to leave a mate posted is the greatest dog act of all.

In fact, the only time I ever saw the stooge act work properly was when the Thomastown, Keon Park, Lalor and Reservoir boys teamed up to fight the Crevelli Street boys from Preston. We used three 14-year-olds as bait and we ambushed the Crevelli Street mob outside the Preston Town Hall.

The fight went from the Town Hall and ended up in the car park of the Preston railway station, then on to the station itself. I was 14 and armed with a cricket bat. Someone yanked it out of my hands and used it on me. Being belted with your own cricket bat is quite humiliating. I ended up with blood in my lungs, and was coughing up and pissing blood for some time. I also had a busted nose, bloodshot eyes, ringing in my ears and fuzzy vision, which lasted about a month. But we all thought we had won the fight, even though one kid from Keon Park had his eyeball pulled out and another two blokes from Reservoir got stabbed in the guts and the groin with broken beer bottles. And a kid from Lalor broke his leg when he jumped off the train on the way home.

It was a great afternoon out.

There was about 60 of us and 20 of them. So for once, the odds were on our side. You always needed three to one odds to fight Crevelli Street, in my opinion.

I lived at 4 Marcia Street, Thomastown, across the road from the Goodyear tyre factory, when we first moved to Thomastown in the late 1950s. At that time there were still farms in the area. A farmer used to herd his cows up the dirt road out the front. It was all dirt roads, open drains and outside dunnies. It wasn't until the 1960s that we got sewerage and push button toilets, and then we thought we were really posh.

I went to Thomastown East State School and Lalor High, and I never won a single fight. Bashing me up was the school hobby. In fact, I think it was on the curriculum. Even if I couldn't win, I always came back for more. They would flog me at school and then wait outside my house for me as I walked home, and then I would get another giant touch-up. But when duty called, I was a Thomastown boy, and I would side with the very boys who would beat me at school. At least it was a change, being beaten up by strangers instead of the blokes you knew.

I would never shirk my civic duty when it came to gang fights and street battles. There was a joke going around at the time that while the other gang was bashing me, my side could make good its escape. That was because I never surrendered. I couldn't fight, but I didn't give up.

The one thing that helped me in all these fights was that I was born with an incredibly hard head. I have now found to my cost that the older you get, the less damage you can afford to the old skull. But as a young bloke, I had a head like a mallet. As a kid I would go swimming at the Preston Pool. I remember once diving into the deep end with my hands by my side. OK, it's not exactly an Olympic diving event, but it was pretty impressive to the bucks in Preston back then. I would just run up and take a flying nose dive into the pool. One time I tried it and my head banged against the skull of another kid in the pool. It felt like an explosion. I jumped out of the pool and looked back to see some poor kid, face down in the water with blood pouring out of a huge wound in his head. Look on the bright side, I thought. At least there's no sharks in the pool.

Other people rushed to the rescue and pulled him out. He was about 16 and I was 13 at the time. I walked quickly to the dressing rooms, got changed and left the area. But as I was going, I saw the ambulance arrive to cart the kid off to hospital. I don't know what happened to him. All I know is that his head gave way, and mine didn't. It's been the story of my life.

I remember when I was expelled from Lalor High and went to a school in Preston, by way of welcome some kid stabbed me in the neck with a compass, and I hit him over the head with the edge of my steel ruler. He ran screaming from the classroom with blood pissing from a half-inch gash in his head. Never mind me, who was sitting in a desk with a hole in the right side of my neck. He could have killed me.

At least the kid stuck solid and, even though he was taken to hospital, he didn't tell the teachers how his head was opened up.

On the way home, I was nursing my neck wound and wondering if moving schools was a good idea, when I was confronted by the bloke's mates.

I always lead with my head and this time was no exception. They held me by the arms and kicked me in the face, neck and eyes, and left me like a bag of shit in the street.

I was back at school the next day, but by now I was starting to get a little smarter. I got each one of the pricks with the perfect sneak go. I waited for each one to be on his own and then got them with a rounders bat.

I then went home, content, even though my head looked like a busted watermelon – but they were waiting for me and I got another head kicking. When I finally dragged myself home, I was flogged for fighting.

Yeah, life was great when I was a kid.

At school, my head was used as a football. I was brave, but stupid. I had courage, but no strategy. But I was prepared to learn. By the time I was 15, I had been on the losing end of several hundred schoolyard punch-ups, gang wars and street fights, plus a good number of sound thrashings at home. By that age I was a seasoned campaigner in matters of violence. I had the experience of a 30-year-old nightclub bouncer.

All of a sudden the wheel started to turn. I started to win fights. Then I met Cowboy Johnny, Dave the Jew and Terry the Tank and formed a gang of my own. Instead of being the victim and punching bag, I was the general of my own army. And what an army it was. The Cowboy looked like death, and fought like the Grim Reaper, the Jew was a kill-crazy, head-banging psychopath, even at that age, and Terry the Tank was a jolly giant, who could punch a German Shepherd dog to death, and once did, to prove a point.

I was leading the mentally ill, but in my own way I was the worst of them all. I had the smiling face of a young angel, and a heart so full of tears that there was no room for the blood to flow. I was emotionally and mentally twisted. As a young guy I was cruel, cold and totally without human mercy, feeling or compassion.

I didn't feel hate. I was just emotionally numb. All I had was my own sense of right and wrong. I saw everything only in terms of battles and strategies. I lived to spill the blood of my enemies, and there were plenty of them.

I am almost gentle and overflowing with human kindness when I look at myself now, compared with what I was. From the age of 15, I was a cruel, cold-blooded, twisted, smiling, sadistic arsehole and, backed up by my crew of young crazies, inflicted as much damage as I possibly could to as many other gang members as I could find.

I was also a young egomaniac on a power trip fed by a blood lust. Let's be honest, as a young bloke I was a sick piece of work. I started to see myself as God-like and all others as sub-human. I mean, my crew thought I was a genius, so I thought I must be.

Let's face it, I was as nutty as a fruit cake. Thank God, I'm all better now.

Ha ha, ha.

CHAPTER 20

RATS ON STILTS RORT RUNS OFF RAILS

'I AM A SUCKER FOR ANY CLOWN
WHO COMES UP TO ME AND TELLS ME
HE HAS A SURE THING'

I SEE myself as the typical Aussie male. Sure, I may be covered in tattoos, have no ears, have a criminal record you can't jump over and torture drug dealers for profit and pleasure, but I personally see those as minor cosmetic differences.

Underneath it all, I am just like the next bloke. I like a laugh, a drink, shooting scumbags and, most of all, when I am on the outside, I like a bet.

I made a bit of a mess of it at the Launceston Casino, winning heaps and then going mad and losing it all, and about 10 times more. I loved it there, but I have never been any good with money and I would lose thousands a night.

I was arrested by Tasmania's finest over the Sid Collins rubbish on the way home from the casino. One of my great regrets is that they didn't arrest me on the way there. That way, at least, I would have been left with a few bucks in my pocket.

If it's not casinos then it is the track which attracts me for a little punt. In the old days it didn't matter. Lose at the track and I'd go out and grab a drug dealer to get a bit more play money. It kept money circulating and was good for the economy. But when you decide to retire in windswept Tassie, give up head hunting and live off the pittance from books and the dole, then the high life is over.

But as a respected author and crime figure, I needed to continue to associate with riff-raff (purely for literary research purposes, you understand) and it was during this that I started to punt again, and in a big way. In fact, I am a sucker for any clown who comes up to me and tells me he has a sure thing.

A few of the boys in Launceston used to go down to the greyhound track called 'White City'. Me and Mad Micky would go down with some others and most times we would lose. But we would have a good time and it was a great laugh.

Young Trent Anthony had his trainer's ticket and we got to know a lot of the main figures at the track – bookies, trainers and punters. In the end I invested in a greyhound with Trent and his grandfather. I was then talked into buying two more. We were going famously and then others at the track told me that sometimes there was such an item as a sure thing and, when it arrived, I would be told in advance and could get in on the giggle. It would be a dead cert, a sure winner, wink, wink. I won't name the parties involved because that wouldn't be nice, but it was a crew of about nine, and a greyhound that was famous for losing. We will call it 'Speedy' although that is not its real name.

The syndicate managed to rake up $15,000, of which $4,000 was mine. It was to be the plunge of the century, in Tassie at least. We covered six bookies and got up to 50 to 1.

As had been predicted, the favourite got scratched that night. Shortly before the race, the fourth on the card, was due to start, someone smelled a rat and Speedy went from rank outsider to even money.

But it didn't worry us, we were already on. I was told Speedy would win and the owner-trainer would probably lose his trainer's licence, as the game would or could be found out, but that he was in deep financial trouble and was prepared to pay the price for one big win. He stood to make $50,000 for the win, enough to make it worthwhile for him. For me, the big win would have set me up. OK, it wasn't the Fine Cotton affair, but it wasn't bad for Launceston.

Speedy was a brindle bitch, and a big one. Even though she was like lightning at trials, she always lost on the night in races because she was timid, meek and very nervous. On the night in question she was given a little backyard medical treatment, so I was led to believe. This would stop the problems of fear.

I never put any money on myself with the bookies, but I ended up holding all the tickets. Off they went like greased lightning, and for three quarters of the race I thought Speedy was going to get up. She was in front by about two metres, and I was already counting my winnings in my head. Then, for no reason at all, she went arse up and fell over, sending about three others running into her.

The rest of the dogs just charged on regardless with some 7–4 on, flea-bitten, cat-chasing thing winning. I thought the whole race should have been declared a non-event. But I would hardly say to the stewards, 'Hey, we had a boat race going on in the fourth, could we declare it a non-race?'

We lost the lot. Needless to say, I was most upset. Two weeks later, I went to visit the numbskull who owned Speedy and I shot the dog in front of him, and made him write me a cheque for $4,000 to repay my loss.

The cheque didn't bounce. Neither did the dog. The fact that the guy had the money to pay me back indicated he wasn't as broke as he had made out, so I am still suspicious about what he was up to. I love animals, but greyhounds aren't pets, they are business, and there is no place in this wide world for a slow greyhound, let alone a frightened one with a drug problem which insists on trying to do back flips in the middle of a race when it is leading and has my money on its skinny back. I've heard people call racing dogs 'rats on stilts' and now I know why.

This was the second time I got cross at a Tassie race meeting.

The other time was when Mike Alexander, the owner of one of the world's great pubs, the Clarendon Arms Hotel in Evandale, along with his girlfriend, Michelle, took me and Sid 'never tell a lie' Collins to a race meeting in Devonport.

Mike owns a small string of race horses, or more like a string of pet food ponies, if you ask me, and one was running this day.

Every tip Mike gave me was a non-event. I had a bookie giving me a few tips too. Bad move, why would a bookie tip you into a winner? He would be drummed off the course for breaking the bookies' code of never giving a sucker an even break.

In the end, I put a roll of dough on Mike Alexander's horse and, needless to say, lost the lot.

I went back after the race, hoping to shoot the bloody animal in the head, but there were too many people around. Mike is a good bloke and a top publican, but he is a worse punter than me. The bloke couldn't pick his nose. He had some good wins, but like me, he is a hopeless punter and we go to the track to commit suicide, not to win.

CHAPTER 21

THE GOOD, THE BAD AND THE DEADSET UNLUCKY

'THE BEST OF THE LOT IS SOME BRAIN-DEAD
JOKER FROM WESTERN AUSTRALIA WHO
HAS WRITTEN TO TELL ME HE IS THE REAL
MARK 'CHOPPER' READ AND THAT I AM JUST
CASHING IN ON HIS REPUTATION'

IF people don't like me they can either kill me or cop it sweet, and until I am in my grave they can stick it as far as I'm concerned. To hell with them all.

Their hatred is like sunshine to me. I thrive on it. There is something about me that seems to inflame hatred and passion in many people. I just don't understand it myself. To me I am just your everyday normal killer, but to others I seem to be the devil in disguise.

It is obvious to me that I am like a magnet to the mentally ill. Now while it is fantastic that my first two books have been well received by the good old Aussie public, there is unfortunately no law about keeping loonies out of book shops and, sadly, these sickos love to put pen to paper and write to me.

I wish I could debate my literary efforts with other respected and well-known authors over a sherry and Greek dip. Instead, I am sure that if I met most of the people who have read my work I would have to ask them to stop weaving their baskets before we could discuss their views on my writing.

I get hate mail from people who claim to be Dave the Jew, Cowboy

Johnny Harris and Terry the Tank. These brain-dead, barking nutters either have the same name or the same nickname as some of the main characters in the books and they then seem to think that I have written about them.

Now, one doesn't need to be a Rhodes Scholar or a former Prime Minister to work out that if you don't know Chopper Read and didn't live in Melbourne in the 1970s and 1980s then I would hardly be writing about you. But these weirdos think I am.

In the second book I wrote about two girlies, Randy Mandy and Midnight. I have been driven nuts by girls around Australia with the same nicknames who have written to me and call me all sorts of things. Such language! It is enough to make a grown gunman blush.

They have suggested that I have made these stories up about them. Well, let's get it clear. The name 'Randy Mandy' was changed by my two alcoholic editors because the woman concerned had a long relationship with a policeman who was before the court at the time. It was feared that using her real name may have put us all in hot water with the County Court. The name was changed to protect the guilty and I end up copping bags of hate mail from bimbos called Mandy.

The nickname 'Midnight' was chosen to protect the dad and mum of the girl I was talking about. I know the old couple well and they are nice people. The real 'Midnight', as I called her, died in the early 1980s from a heroin overdose.

So to the Randy Mandys and Midnights of the world who keep writing me these jelly bean letters, leave me alone and get yourself a life.

There is also some ratbag called Freddy the Wog who keeps writing to me claiming I have said awful things about him. Must I remind these people that I am a person of great patience, tolerance and good humour, just ask Sammy the Turk. But when pushed I can sometimes get a little cranky, so please stop writing these sorts of letters to me.

The best one is some brain-dead joker from Western Australia who has written to tell me he is the real 'Chopper' Read and that I am just cashing in on his reputation.

Just think of it for a moment. There is a bloke in WA who thinks he is me and believes that he chopped his ears off, shot Sammy the Turk, has been given life on the bum rap of shooting some two-bob bikie in Launceston and has spent most of his life in jail.

I hope he's right and that the jail authorities have got the wrong bloke in the bin. If this clown wants to come over here and swap places with me I would be delighted. I would even take the medication that I'm sure he must be on.

The mentally ill seem to find their way to my door. I really seem to boil the buggers up. I wonder what Cowboy Johnny would say if he knew that he really wasn't dead and was alive and well and living in South Australia.

One letter I got was from two dream boats who wanted to put on a play based on my life at La Mama Theatre in Lygon Street, Carlton. I didn't know what to file that under. Could you imagine that? The Dagos would burn the place down on opening night.

I find it an interesting lesson in human nature that I have gotten a large number of letters from good, concerned people from around Australia. They seem to be decent folk and they all include their return addresses. Yet when you get the big, rough tough individual who wants to have a go at me, or make some idle threat about my wellbeing, in their rage, they all forget to include the important fact of where they live.

Some of them may be mad, but none of them are totally stupid. Oh well, what goes around comes around. One day I may bring a new meaning to the term Dead Letter Office.

WELL, it had to happen sooner or later. I am now dying of AIDS, according to the latest gossip, no doubt as a result of not washing my hands after going to the toilet. Yes, according to the rumours, I am

234

HIV positive. I suppose it was only a matter of time. I knew that if I kept hanging around public toilets, dressed in my granny's wedding dress and my mum's high heels, I was playing with fire.

Let that be a lesson for me, slap me on my limp wrist and call me Gomer Pile. Yes, I am a police informer, nancy boy, weak prick who can't fight, Elvis impersonator, a basher of small children and young girls, a poof dying of AIDS, Adolf Hitler's love child and a lousy tipper.

I have traced some of these rumours down to some known enemies of mine in the Outlaw motorcycle gang. These rumours seem to jump Bass Strait and end up back in the mainland.

We have had a laugh in Risdon when the latest one came back that I was given a sound flogging from my mate, Rocky Devine. Another one was that I was given a kicking by Shane Hutton and he bit off a piece of my nose. Well, I hope he rushes of to have a blood test to see if I've given him AIDS.

The rumours fly thick and fast. I am supposed to have taken a $20,000 contract out on Crown witness Trent Anthony. To be frank, I wouldn't give you the deposit on a Coke bottle for that worm. I am supposed to be dying, deaf in one ear, wear contact lenses and have been bashed by more people than I can name. There is a rumor that I am dead. Maybe James Dean, Buddy Holly, Elvis and me can form a rock band. We would call ourselves The Good, The Bad and The Deadset Unlucky.

Things have never been the same since I left Krypton.

I SHOULD be flattered by the rumours. It means that while I am inside, at least I am not forgotten. People just love rumours, never let the facts stand in the way of a good gossip, they say. People even ring radio stations to spread them.

Remember when the late Prime Minister, Harold Holt, drowned while swimming off Portsea beach? The rumours started that he was kidnapped by the CIA, then by the Peking secret police. Gives a new meaning to the term 'Chinese takeaway', doesn't it?

I have heard that hitman Christopher Dale 'Rentakill' Flannery is not really dead, but living in Canada. I understand that Victorian police launched a secret operation to trap my old mate, the escapee, armed robber and curry fiend 'Mad Dog', in his secret hideout at Phillip Island in 1987. Now he was the master of disguises, but after the coppers had interviewed 50 fairy penguins and 200 Japanese tourists they realised they had missed their man. Mad Dog later told me he had never been to Phillip Island.

Police and the underworld thrive on rumours. At one stage, Mad Dog and I were going to gun each other down on sight. Except for the time he tried to kill me with the hottest jail curry in the world in Pentridge, we have always been the best of friends.

There was another rumour that a policeman was behind the murder of Ray Chuck in the Melbourne Magistrates' Court. Well, knock me down with an Irish potato and call me baldy if that one is true.

CHAPTER 22

JESUS MENZIES COMES TO JAIL

'WHEN I MET JOHN AGAIN, HE WAS
NO LONGER JESUS CHRIST … HE TOLD
ME HE WAS THE REINCARNATION OF
SIR ROBERT MENZIES'

IF Jesus, the son of God, came down to earth in the 20th century and walked the streets of Melbourne or Sydney, blessing people, healing the sick and turning water into wine, he would be arrested immediately and declared a crackpot.

It was in Royal Park Mental Hospital that I met the Lord. He walked up and introduced himself as Jesus Christ. It was obvious to me that this version of old JC had been turning water into metho and then partaking of the product in no uncertain manner, and it had got the better of him.

He gave his name to one and all as Jesus Christ. However, in deeper moments, he did tell me that the first time he realised that he was different was in Vietnam in 1967. It was during a gun battle and he threw his gun down and walked away, he told me. It was a noble gesture except he headed in the wrong direction and, instead of heading to safety, walked smack bang into the line of fire.

After telling me this he lifted his shirt to show me a hole in his stomach the size of a fist and a massive scar and hole in his lower back about the same size.

He told me that while he was lying on the wet Vietnamese earth, convinced he was dying, the thought that he was Jesus Christ seized him.

I will simply call this man John. Some years after I first met John in the Royal Park Mental Hospital, I met him again in G Division, Pentridge. It was the area kept in jail for the mentally unwell. I had obviously been put there by mistake, ha ha. I was actually sent there after I mislaid my ears. Obviously, those in power thought this was not the act of a well unit.

When I met John again, he was no longer Jesus Christ. However, he walked around the division with a Bible in his hand and was very Christ-like in his speech. He told me he was the reincarnation of former Liberal Prime Minister, Sir Robert Menzies. Thank goodness he was not English and decided he was Margaret Thatcher. I don't think her beehive haircut would have gone down too well in the boob.

John told me that all the cell numbers were wrong: 22 should have been 23, 23 should have been 24, and so on. Now our jailhouse version of Bobby Menzies was a doer, not a talker, so he got a small paintbrush and changed all the numbers in the division.

In one of John's past lives when he was in the army, someone had taught him either unarmed combat or karate. For the rest of us, this was not good. A clearly deranged man who was also very handy with his hands and feet was not that comforting to have around. John was a nasty fellow when he was put out, and he would sometimes jump high in the air and throw a kick that would put Bruce Lee to shame.

He decided that a drinking fountain in the exercise yard was possessed by the Devil and no one was to drink from it. John, or should I say, Sir Robert, stood guard each day when he was let out of his cell. For nearly two weeks Sir Robert stood guard at the water tap, threatening anyone who came near him with the wrath of God.

I was more than 18 stone at the time with 18$^{1/2}$inch arms and a neck to match. I had got into body building and weight work in jail in a big way. I was bench pressing 330 pounds in sets of 21, 21 times a day. I was pretty strong. On one particular day I was trying to bench press 400 pounds when John walked past. He snatched the bar bell with the 400-pound weight, picked it up over his head and tossed it against the wall. He was as skinny as a rake and not a physically well man, but had blazing eyes and a mind that truly believed he was some sort of messenger from God.

He may have been mad but his mind was his strength. John was in his element in G Division as all the inmates and half the staff were mad. Another prisoner in G Division pulled his own eye out with his fingers. They would slash themselves with razor blades and run around the yard bleeding like taps.

I learned amongst that madness that everything counts on the mind ... the mind controls all. No swordsmanship, however just, can stand secure against a madman's thrust.

I ran that division like the King of England, because I became an expert in dealing with the mad. They believed me to be some sort of God and I did not go out of my way to persuade them that they were wrong. Even some of the crazies who felt they were God acknowledged me as a God as well. In the end there were so many 'Gods' in G Division it was like a religious convention.

I used to steal all the maddies' tobacco and other assorted goodies, then lend it back to them. The whole Division was deep in debt to me. I was the G Division Benevolent Dictator.

There was one chap there who had killed his mother and then taken her to bed. No sex, mind you, just a cuddle. That's how police found him two days later, cuddling his mother in the cot.

He would walk past me in jail and say, 'Chopper, it was never like this in Mt Beauty', whatever that meant. This fellow was also a homosexual. I took a dislike to him and I let Sir Robert know that this little mother-killer was not only a messenger from Satan, but a communist homosexual and that I had heard him speak ill of Dame Pattie, Sir Robert's beloved wife.

Naturally, while Sir Robert would have forgiven all the problems of the guy, the insults against Dame Pattie could not be left unanswered. Sir Robert got a bucket and went to the G Division kitchen, filled it with boiling water, then wandered the division until he found the Mummy's boy and, splash, Sir Robert gave him the boiling bath.

It was a painful thing to watch. When Mummy's boy came back from hospital he glared at me, but I told Sir Robert to keep a close eye on him. I also had a mob of mentally ill inmates who were proud to be in Chopper's Army. I knew I was safe. While the Mummy's boy was no physical threat to me, he would kill you as quick as look at you. In the world of life and death how big and strong you are or how well you can fight plays no role whatsoever.

About a week after the return of Mummy's boy, I was having a shower alone, having dismissed my whacked-out crew of body-guards, when I saw the mad killer approaching. He had taken me by surprise. I thought the shower area had been locked off. He pulled out a butcher's knife from under his coat and walked slowly towards me with a confused look on his face. This looked like being the remake of the shower scene from Psycho. He was angry and frightened, and that is a bad combination in an enemy.

I had no place to run. He had me cornered, so I just said to him, 'You were never like this in Mt Beauty,' and he stopped dead and said, 'No, no, it was never like this in Mt Beauty.'

I then said, 'Is that your knife?'

He said, 'No.' I said, 'Is that for me?' and he said, 'Yes.' I put my hand out and said 'Give it to me then.' He handed it to me and I thanked him. I then said, 'This is not my knife, this looks like your mother's knife.' He started to cry and I said, 'Here, you take this and give it to your mother.' He said that he didn't know where his mother was and I said, 'Mt Beauty.'

He then slashed his own arm with the butcher's knife in front of me, screamed and fell to the ground. Sir Robert Menzies rushed in to the shower area to see what was wrong and on seeing Mummy's boy on the shower block floor, bleeding and crying, Sir Robert pointed at him and screamed, 'You will not be forgiven' and proceeded to kick the writhing form on the ground.

I said to Sir Robert, 'He was never like this in Mt Beauty.' Sir Robert replied, 'I'll give the bastard Mt Beauty.'

By this time, the screws had arrived and I wrapped a towel around me and walked out, leaving them all to it.

There is a skill in dealing with the mentally ill, and I have always had a natural flair in this regard. But I don't know whether that is a compliment or an insult.

I still haven't lost the ability. I will give you an example. There was a young bloke in the remand yard here in Risdon who was running around Launceston, Devonport and later, Hobart, telling people he was my son. He just seemed to have this thing about me. I have always drawn nutters like a magnet. He came to jail for insanity rather than crime, a real lost and hopeless case.

He would walk up to me and say, 'Chopper, can I have a smoke?' I'd say, 'No, piss off, go away from me.' He would go away, sit down and cry. About 10 minutes later I would soften, call him over and give him a smoke, then I would say, 'Now piss off, you bloody numbnut.' He would walk away beaming like a smiling machine.

Keep a mad person confused on a tight rope between anger and kindness and you keep them fascinated. I could have given the ratbag a knife and told him to kill the Governor and he would have done it, because he feared and loved me at the same time.

The way you train a whacko is the way you train a dog, easy as pie. Although, to tell the truth, I have found there is not that much difference between the mentally ill and the so-called normal world.

People generally respond better to kindness after you have scared the shit out of them. People and puppies are a lot alike.

A puppy really appreciates a pat and a cuddle after a swift kick.

Why do some women insist on staying with men who bash the shit out of them? When the man shows kindness, they come back. Crazy, isn't it?

Of course, every walking individual is different and there are contradictions to every rule and everyone is a walking contradiction. The only rule which has stood the test of time for me is that all people are slightly mad and the more people I meet, the more I am convinced of this fact.

There is no such thing as total sanity. We are all slightly insane; it is just that some of us hide it better than others. The ones we consider are mad are really just slightly madder than the rest of the world, and that is just a judgement call.

Talk to a psychiatrist or psychologist and you will see what I mean. These two groups of people are proof positive that the mentally ill can masquerade as totally normal and get away with it.

It is all in the mind, whatever that is.

CHAPTER 23

THE SHOOTING OF SIDNEY

'THE OPERA AIN'T OVER TILL
SOMEONE SHOOTS THE FAT LADY'

IN 1992, before my arrest on the Collins shooting, wherever I went I had young Trent Anthony with me, carrying my gun. It was Tassie, and I was safe, but that was no reason to become lazy or allow myself to be caught napping. Graveyards are full of people who dropped their guards. Not even Trent's best friend would describe him as a heavy thinker, but he was a first class fetch and carry boy, and a wonderful lackey. He waited on me hand and foot, collected me in the morning, drove me here, there and everywhere. I would use him for target practice, getting him to hold targets in his hands from various distances while I took pot shots.

In the lackey department, Trent was first rate. However, he proved a total failure in a police station. I think it is safe to say he will never get his job back now. I also think it is time to tell the true story of how Sid Collins was shot.

I didn't witness the actual shooting, but I knew that Sid had an appointment with a bullet – it was just a matter of when. Why did I know this? Because Sid had his own enemies. He had already asked me to kill one of them, a former Outlaw motorcycle heavy. I refused the request, but soon after was approached by a man with the offer to shoot Sid. It was all too much. Sid was creating big bother and was going to get shot, pure and simple. It was always just a matter of where and who would be the trigger man.

I was interested in watching what happened, but I wanted no part of the gunplay. Everyone knew that Sid and I got around together. I knew that any shooting in Launceston would come back to me. I was consulted re Sid and on a purely hypothetical basis, mind you, was asked my professional opinion on what would be the best weapon. I advised the interested party that the .410 sawn-off shotgun was an old favourite. I was told that Sid was only going to be shot in the leg as a warning. As much as I tried to keep out of it, I was being dragged into Sid's coming misfortune, whether I liked it or not.

I wasn't pleased, and I spoke harshly to the bloke who intended to shoot Collins. But mainly, I wanted to know when the deed was going to be done. I added that what he did when I was at the casino was his business.

If it was to happen I wanted to be sure I had an alibi because I knew the police would be looking at me. When the would-be tough guy came back with another bloke he said it had all gone wrong and he had changed his mind. I abused both of them as a pair of two-bob gangsters and to stop trying to involve me in bullshit. I told the nitwit who wanted me to shoot Sid that if he ever mentioned the matter to me again I would shoot him instead. That was about a week before Sid really did cop one in the guts. When I heard he had been shot, it didn't take me long to figure out what had happened and who had done it.

On 13 May 1992, I had been drinking with Sid. Trent and I dropped him off at number 17, High Street, Evandale, after a light-hearted and happy drinking session at the Clarendon Arms Hotel with mine host, Micky Alexander.

I'd just given Sid $1,300 to help pay for his girlfriend's wedding dress. All was well. The talk of who was going to shoot who was all in the past. After waving Sid goodbye, Trent took me to the casino. I was far more interested in shooting craps than shooting Sid at the time.

Trent left to go back to Evandale. When he came back for me he told me Sid had burst his appendix and that he had driven him to hospital. Naturally, as anyone would, I found this the height of good humour – for Sid to bust his gut a week before he was due to be married. The thought of the wedding night would make anyone laugh. Trent and I left the casino and it was then we blew a welsh plug in my car and pulled into a petrol station for repairs.

We left the car and caught a cab back to the casino. I was still questioning Trent about Sid's tummy troubles. The cab driver even joined in on the joke about Sid's burst appendix. Had I shot Sid, I would hardly have been chattering about Trent taking Sid to hospital while we were in the taxi, where the bloody cab driver could hear every word. This was a small point that was obviously missed by the jury. When I was told that Sid had been shot, I naturally suspected the .410 shotty had been used. When I was grabbed by the police, I suspected it. I knew I would be the first cab off the rank. But when the police mentioned the word Beretta, I suspected I was in trouble. I could smell 'set-up' from the word go. Sid jumped on the bandwagon, then the police found the Beretta that was used in my back yard. It was the same Beretta Sid had given me as a gift.

I know the man who pulled the trigger, but I won't name him, as it is not the done thing. Sid and Trent wanted me out of the way and in jail. There were other factors. I don't like drugs, but it was rumoured that Sid did not have the same opposition to the illicit product as I did. Foul gossip, I am sure.

I didn't shoot Sid Collins. It would have been the lime funeral, not a hospital bed if I had. Margaret and I were planning to get married in June, so even I wouldn't be shooting people in May. I don't know why they decided to set me up with the crime. Maybe some people were frightened of me. Maybe they thought I would be easy to blame, and maybe some people wanted me out of the way so they could deal in drugs. I am still puzzled.

Pumping a slug into someone's leg or guts is no big deal in Melbourne or Sydney. If Sid needed a shot in the guts to teach him to pull up his socks, it was none of my concern. He was a mate, but if he was putting a hole in his manners, that was his lookout. But why blame me? Maybe someone told Sid I was behind it all, or maybe I was just a convenient scapegoat. I will probably never know.

As for teaching Sid to pull his socks up, I could have told them that you can't teach a bloke to pull up his socks if he's wearing thongs, mentally speaking.

As for Trent Anthony: you can't put bow ties on Billy goats.

I don't know. Sunk by nitwits for the only one I didn't do. Then again, for the ones I've got away with I'm still well in front. What a twisted comedy.

ONE very important legal point that people forget about me is that when I am guilty of a crime and the police arrest me, I say, 'Yeah, so what', and I freely admit to what I have done. To me it is a game and if you are caught, then it is no use howling and pretending that you are some whiter than white saint who has never done the wrong thing. Many crims eventually convince themselves that they didn't do it, even when they are caught with the smoking gun in their hands and there are 100 witnesses prepared to swear that they saw the bloke pull the trigger.

I am not like that. If I did it and I am caught, then it's a fair cop and you do the time without complaining. There are tons of crimes that I got away with over the years and have never been arrested for, but that is another story.

The point is, if the police arrest me on a charge I am guilty of, I plead guilty. But if the police arrest me on a charge of which I am innocent, then I will plead not guilty. The rape charge in 1975 was one I didn't do. I pleaded not guilty and the lady got up in court and said: 'No, Chopper never raped me. It was Mad Charlie.'

The shooting I was charged with in 1987 was in self-defence so I pleaded that and beat the murder charge. Now we have the Sid Collins shooting. I didn't do it and I will never plead guilty.

I will never surrender. I will fight on in the face of unbeatable odds. I simply will not plead guilty to a crime that I simply did not do. Why should I? Would you? I think not. So why should I be forced to plead guilty on a matter I didn't do just because I am a career criminal.

> For all the wars of man and men,
> Fought on a blood soaked field,
> Facing dragons in the rising sun,
> But I will never yield.
> I stood alone in Doomsday's door,
> With no man to hold my shield,
> Facing death a thousand fold,
> And still I would not yield.
> For the sake of the widow's son,
> I face the Goliath Beast,
> And by God and King Billy
> I slew the Satan's Priest,
> And the wise men and the cautious
> Shed tears as I fell,
> And when the reaper called my name,
> They shut the gates to Hell,
> And so I went on up to Heaven
> And God said, Sorry, my gates are sealed,
> So I dwell alone in nothing land,
> But still I will not yield.

I've been a crook or a long, long time, but in my own way, I have been an honest crook. I will stand up and say yes, I did that, and I did this, but I didn't do the other. I expect to be believed.

Bloody hell, I can't be guilty of everything. Can I?

THE barrister doing my appeal was a Mr Greg Richardson, recommended to me by Anita Betts. If I win a re-trial Anita will be back defending me. But for the appeal she felt a fresh legal mind was needed, and in keeping with strict Tasmanian tradition, we decided to keep it in the family.

Greg Richardson is Anita's ex-husband. He is also one of Tassie's top courtroom brawlers. When I first met Greg he reminded me of a cross between a used car dealer and an over-the-hill nightclub bouncer. There was a touch of Collingwood about his personality, and once we started talking I knew at once he was a no-holds-barred courtroom streetfighter, and that's what I needed for the appeal.

I suspect Greg likes to play the role of the small town country lawyer, but the grand-a-day retainer and the Armani suit pokes a rather large hole in the little charade. Gregory Peck in To Kill A Mockingbird he definitely isn't. He is a rough diamond with plenty of dash. I needed a tough man for the appeal, not some old school tie 'if your Honour pleases' faggot who is only in it for the money and not the result.

I'd rather have a lawyer shake your hand with the slight odour of Canadian Club Whisky about his person than reeking of Chanel No 5. I have met my fair share of (how can I say this politely?) screaming queens in the legal profession.

There is one big deal lawyer in Tassie, who I cannot name, who rang Anita trying to get my appeal. No doubt he was a bit anxious to get his name back into the headlines. The only way to describe the bloke would be to call him the fairy at the bottom of the garden.

One of the old school tie Mafia, recommended to all the accused by the police.

But I have my reputation to consider and I will not be represented by limp-wristed drama queens and legal bum boys, no matter how good they are or think they are.

Greg Richardson came highly recommended by a wide assortment of local cut-throats and killers. Mad Micky Marlow speaks very highly of him and I like Greg's style. He is a man's man, which is rare in the rather effeminate world of the legal fraternity.

We ended up losing the appeal, but I won't bag the poor bugger.

That's not my style. Only mugs and poor sports blame their bloody lawyers.

I THOUGHT that before I give a day-to-day account of the legal battle that lies ahead, I should inform the reader about my arch enemy and the man who has placed me in my present legal dilemma, the one and only Tasmanian Director of Public Prosecutions, Mr Damian Bugg.

Now the Buggster is one cool customer. He walks into court followed by various cup bearers, including a young, well-educated lass with a honeysuckle face. She must have been very good at her schoolwork to get where she is.

Buggsy is prematurely grey, no doubt from doing legal battle with the forces of evil, including my good self. I fear that at times, Damian may take himself a tad too seriously when he attacks me so violently. But if goodness is its own reward, then I am sure the Buggster will be well satisfied in another place.

I am in two minds about him. It has been said that a man can be judged by the quality of his enemies. If that is the case, then both Damian and I must be top-quality chaps.

'And now the time has come,' the walrus said, 'when all things will be revealed.'

Tuesday, 1 June 1993

WELL, after more delays than I would care to mention, my legal appeal over the Sid Collins nonsense finally kicked off today. It was supposed to start on 24 May but for assorted reasons it was delayed until today.

Their Honours, Justice Zeeman, Wright and Crawford were in the driver's seat. Mr Greg Richardson was representing my good self and, as always, the master of mirth, Delightful Damian Bugg, was atop his white charger (the horse, not the car) fighting for truth, justice and the Tasmanian way. The Buggster looked quite dashing as he lined up for the Crown as the reigning champion and local Director of Public Prosecutions.

A motley and somewhat odious looking collection of sticky beaks, retards, courtroom groupies, scallywags and scoundrels, not to mention the clan of giggling half-wits who sit in court waving copies of my book at me, were ready to watch all the legal jibbing and tacking before the three wise wigged ones.

There were a few familiar and friendly faces amongst the giggling crowd in the public gallery. There was Mary-Ann, the chick from the Tax Office, Crazy Joe and Big Bill Watson, a good old boy, as our American friends say. My leggy lawyer, Anita Betts, was also sitting in the public area. It was quite odd to see her there, a little removed from all the legal action.

All the esteemed members of the press were there, all looking serious, with their 'We hate Chopper Read and we ain't gonna smile' looks on.

They're a funny lot, most of the press – in public, they look as though they reckon I should get the death penalty, and would like to flick the switch. Yet in private, they suck up to me something fierce. How they love to pretend to hate me.

Whenever I appear in court it is an extravaganza bordering on farce. An appeal is meant to be all law points and legal argument, dry as dust really. Personalities and emotions are supposed to play no part.

Greg Richardson is as good as his reputation as a sharp professional. According to the rules of play we are allowed to bat first, and Greg gets stuck in and bats all day long.

On the wall behind the three Supreme Court judges is the Tasmanian coat of arms. There is a large wooden lion on the right-hand side and a unicorn on the left. Both are rising up on their hind legs, guarding some sort of smaller coat of arms in the shape of a shield, under this are the Latin words DIEU ET MON DROIT.

I don't know what it means, but if some of the numbnuts sitting in the back of the court are any indication, it should read: 'Thalidomide: yum, yum, we love it.'

2 June

DAY two of my appeal. My lawyer, Mr Greg Richardson, is still battling away, on his feet all day long. Their Honours, Mr Justice Zeeman, Wright and Crawford appear somewhat confused, amused and bemused by Greg's legal arguments, but they don't look terribly convinced.

At this stage I wouldn't bet money on my chances of winning this appeal. His Honour, Mr Justice Zeeman, asks the most questions and he seems to have a bad cold or a touch of the 'flu, because he pulls out an old, war-torn hankie from under his gown, and blows his nose at regular intervals. I have timed these blows at between 20 and 25 minutes apart. His Honour has a very reliable nose.

A local famous political identity; nicknamed 'The Mouth From The South', Mr Michael Hodgeman, came in to watch proceedings today. Mick is a top courtroom punch-on artist in his own right. He sat behind Damian Bugg and Buggsy got out of his chair and went and sat with 'The Mouth' and they had a little chat. The sad thing was that I had always admired Mr Hodgeman. But a man is always judged by the company he keeps, and here he was taking sides with the prosecution.

There is a local tradition amongst lawyers appearing at the Hobart Supreme Court that I call the 'courtroom two step'. Whenever TV camera crews are seen hovering around outside the court the lawyers get ready. When the luncheon adjournment arrives, barristers can be seen racing out of the court and up and down the Supreme Court steps, in the hope of getting their starved heads in on the action.

It is not unusual to find the lawyers quite out of breath after the luncheon adjournment. There is one well-known gun lawyer from Launceston who is famous for the courtroom two step, popping his head up in front of the TV cameras like 'Dicky Knee'.

Bloody lawyers, they're a class act, aren't they? The game continues.

3 June

THE third, and last day of my appeal. Their Honors, Justices Zeeman, Wright and Crawford, have reserved their decisions, so now we play the waiting game, until they come back with the good or bad news.

Greg Richardson did a top job and I can only thank him and praise his efforts. Come what may, he is a good style of a bloke and a bloody top lawyer.

I am relieved to report that Mr Justice Zeeman seems to have recovered from his cold overnight, as there was no appearance today of the offending hankie. I was glad of that, for both our sakes. It is not his fault, but in my view a man in a wig honking into a hankie every 20 to 25 minutes while you are trying to put detailed and complex legal arguments can be a little off-putting.

The only trouble is, I think I caught his cold. I feel like shit while

I am writing this on a cold winter's night. I don't know if they call this place Van Dieman's Land or Van bloody-freezing land.

I was wearing my lucky slip-on shoes that Mad Charlie gave me in 1987, a pair of jeans that Big Bill Watson gave me, a shirt that Margaret gave me and a sports jacket that 'Al Plonko Ferris' gave me. I felt like Secondhand Rose, sitting in the dock. In this gear, I know that I have lost a lot of weight since I was last out.

I think that Greg Richardson may have them on a small legal point. I don't want to get my hopes up, but we may win this. If I get the breaks on this one, it will still be a photo finish.

All is not lost. And if I do lose here, then I'll give it a run in the High Court of Australia.

The Buggster is conducting himself in a very civil manner. It was, 'Yes, Greg. No, Greg. Pardon me, Greg.' And so on. I went down to the cells and the screws put on a tasty lunch of toasted tomato, meat, pepper and chilli sandwiches, washed down with hot coffee.

After lunch, I got down on my knees and prayed: 'Dear Lord, please call the wrath of God down on the heads of Sid Collins and Trent Anthony, and their children and their children's children, and so forth.'

I don't know if it will work or not, but it certainly makes me feel a whole lot better.

You never know, he may help me.

If God loves a sinner, he must really love me. Ha, ha.

June 6

AS I WALK up and down the remand yard at Risdon, awaiting the decisions of their Honours, Mr Justice Zeeman, Wright and Crawford, Psalm 23, verse four keeps coming into my head. 'Yea, though I walk through the valley of the shadow of death, I will fear no evil, for the Lord is with me, his rod and his staff, they comfort me.'

Like a lot of classic nutters I do tend to invoke the name of God. My strict Seventh Day Adventist upbringing is forever coming back to haunt me. Whenever I enter the field of physical combat, I always recite a verse from the Book of Psalms out of the Bible. 'Blessed be the Lord, my rock, who teaches my hands to wage war and my fingers to do battle.' – Psalm 144, verse one. But my favourite is Psalm 59, verse one: 'Deliver me from my enemies, oh my God, keep me away from those who rise against me.'

The old rocker and roller, Mr Jerry Lee Lewis was quoted as saying that his head was in heaven, but his heart was in hell.

Well, that old killer and me have that much in common. The devil sits on one shoulder, and God on the other, and I guess I will never shake it.

I know that I outrage and anger a lot of so-called Christians. They ask how a monster like me can invoke the name of God and dare to believe that I have God on my side.

Well, I know that I do and the opinion of others means little or nothing to me. I am not a Christian or a Bible-basher, I'm just a bloke who believes that when the shit hits the fan, the Lord sees me as the lesser of two evils. Even if God is angry at me, he usually is a damn sight more pissed off with the other buggers I am fighting with at the time.

Guts, Guns and God. In the end, that is all I have going for me. And in the end, that is all any man really needs.

As far as I am concerned, it is a great pity Sid Collins and Trent Anthony didn't read the bible, Exodus 20, Verse 16. 'Thou shall not bear false witness.'

Come on God, get me out of this. Ha ha.

26 June

WELL, the month of June is drawing to a close and the three wise men of the Tasmanian Supreme Court are still considering my appeal. We are now in the dead of winter and if you have never experienced a Risdon Prison winter, then you don't fully understand the meaning of the word cold.

The jail rests in a sort of a valley surrounded by hills which are covered in snow in winter and it is bitterly cold. It looks like the set from The Sound of Music. God, Julie Andrews must have frozen her tits off on that one.

It snowed here the other day and I stood in the remand yard with snow fluttering down and landing on my head, face and shoulders. I put my tongue out and caught a snowflake. The little snowfall lasted only 10 minutes, but it was a first-time jail experience for me, and would have been quite beautiful, if it hadn't been for the fact I had worn a hole in my right shoe and my two pairs of socks had got wet. My right foot was numb with cold and the left one had gone out in sympathy.

At least I got to go inside when Karen (the White Dove) came to visit me. She now uses the bus to get here rather than her thumb, or at least that is what she tells me. I asked if there was anything I could do for her, or if there was anything she wanted, as her birthday was quite near. She put the bite on me for a lawn mower, so I fixed her up with a new lawn mower. Now I have spent a not-so-small fortune on chicks over the years, but she is the first one who ever put the hard word on me for a lawn mower.

My lawyer Anita's offsider, Peter Warmbrunn, came to see me after doing some shopping on my behalf. He must have been in a philosophical mood because he asked, 'What motivates you, Chopper?'

It was a deep question which deserved a deep answer. I thought for a while and then put my hand on his shoulder. 'What motivates me is Irish whisky, sawn-off shotguns and dirty girls.'

Peter stood there for a while and said, 'Yeah, I guess that would motivate anyone,' then looked at me as if I was a complete mental case, not sure if I was joking or serious. The funny thing is that I'm not sure either.

I have been doing a little bit of legal research and even if I lose this appeal, I think the High Court will listen sympathetically to my case. They are not very keen on majority verdict convictions, and that is the way poor Chop Chop went down on this one.

One way or another I will fight on and win this. I will never surrender. I didn't do it and I'm buggered if I am going to bend over and drop my pants for these mice.

Meanwhile, I sit in the remand yard catching snowflakes with my tongue.

Ahh, it's a great life. What a bloody disaster.

27 June

MY OLD mate Big Bill Watson came in to see me today. Big Billy has been very loyal to me since I went into the Pink Palace. He said that it was all over town that I would win the appeal. In fact, he said 'the word around the traps,' was that I would win.

What a strange expression that is. What it really means is that half the drunken lunatics in Hobart, who have nothing better to do, have spent their days gossiping about whether I will get out. These dream merchants' and cretins' only knowledge of the law and crime would be when they are arrested occasionally on drunk and disorderly charges.

'Around the traps' is an expression used to describe what happens when big noters and wishful thinkers get together for a Saturday night piss-up.

But it was good to see Big Billy, and I got a giggle when he told me that if I won and walked free, that he intended to kidnap me and take me to some nightclub in Hobart and introduce me to the biggest and baddest bunch of strippers in town. I have heard about these young ladies and, if reports are correct, I could see myself suffering a physical injury.

Mary-Ann, the lady from the Tax Department, also wants to see me, if I am lucky enough to walk free, and I know for a fact that the White Dove has hatched plans for me which could leave a bloke in a wheelchair before morning.

But I also got a message from an old mate I shall call Johnny Z, who is a master gunsmith. He would also like to see me on my first night out. The thing about being in my late 30s is that I am no longer filled with the youthful madness that hits young blokes, as in: 'Who will I plonk first when I get out of jail?' To quote my old dad: 'Women come and women go, but the love of a good gunsmith lasts forever.'

So, if God does smile on me and my prayers are answered, my first night out will be spent with a bottle of Irish whisky, in front of an open fire with Johnny the gunsmith. First things are first and one must never stand up a good gunsmith, although I must admit that Big Bill's strippers don't sound half bad. As Dave the Jew always says, if you are going to spend money, you may as well buy in bulk.

5 July

I WAS all set to go back to the Supreme Court today to appear before the Master of the Supreme Court over a criminal injuries compensation claim, or hearing, lodged by guess who? Sid 'never tell a lie' Collins and his wife Simone, that's who.

I received a note that if the Crown had to hand over any cash to Sorry Sid and company then the Crown would try and recover the money from me. Let me simply say that in my whole life no one has ever recovered any money from me.

Well, didn't Anita spit the dummy when she heard about this. She ranted and kicked items of office furniture and told the Crown in no uncertain terms that this was not on and we would fight the matter vigorously.

Mind you, while all this bullshit was going on, my appeal was still being considered. So, in my view, any suggestion of me paying compensation is a wee bit premature on Sid's part.

We were all set to get in for some serious legal body and head shots when the call came through that I was not needed and they would sling Sid his compo, and no attempt would be made to recover it from my good self. That was the good news and I take it as a small victory.

As for Sid, his health can't be that crook, for my spies tell me that he has launched into a major keep-fit campaign and health programme. He has turned into just another middle-aged hoon searching for the fountain of youth. I can only wish him well and when he finds the fountain, with any luck he might find his missing kidney floating in it.

As for his nice new compo cheque? I know Simone, his new wife, quite well, and I am confident that she will have that little lot spent in no time flat.

No, 1992 certainly wasn't Sid's year. He got shot and married. He managed to keep a straight face while giving Crown evidence in my first two trials, but let's see how he goes if there is a re-trial. This fight is far from over.

11 July

STILL no word on the appeal. I suspect I probably won't get an answer until August. Oh well. Que sera sera, whatever will be, will be. I bet when Doris Day sang those lovely words, she wasn't facing life in the bin for allegedly shooting some dirt bag would-be bikie named Sid Collins.

But I digress.

Mary-Ann came in to see me again today, and I was surprised to learn that she was also born into a strict Seventh Day Adventist family, and left the church in her late teens. She used to go to the same church my mother still attends. It is indeed a small world.

I got a letter from 'Sherrie Sinatra', the bad girl of ladies' wrestling. I met her years ago at Bojangles Nightclub in St Kilda. She was one tough chick and a nice lady. I got another letter wishing me well from a lady kick boxer, named Gloria, from Brisbane. She trains six young girls in kick boxing and they call themselves Chopper's Angels. Isn't that cute?

My little mate Tauree wrote to me to say she had my motto 'Je Ne Regrette Rien' tattooed on her bum. It is really good to see the cultural effect my literary works are having on the general public. They are going where no work has gone before.

I don't know whether it is strange or not but I have always had comical dreams and a lot of my dreams relate to either being shot by a member of the clergy, having dinner with a big rabbit or my various courtroom adventures.

The dinner with the big rabbit dreams have plagued me since childhood. It relates to my mother giving my pet rabbit away to some Greek people and the buggers eating it. The courtroom dreams are quite insane. I keep seeing Sammy The Turk giving evidence against me in the Collins shooting trial and Boris Kayser rushes into the court yelling, 'Your Honour, your Honour, this man is dead. Will the Prosecution stop at nothing?'

I wonder if this dream means that Collins will join Sammy the Turk.

Gee, I hope so.

July 21

THE weather in the remand yard has turned vicious. The person who invented the expression, 'I hope you fry in hell,' has obviously never been to Her Majesty's Prison, Risdon, for there is no doubt that hell is cold, and this is it.

I have some sort of fever and I am sure I have frostbite of both feet. My eyes ache and my head is humming away like a mad lady's vibrator. I feel like shit and I am sure that death is on hand.

> Oh wrap me in my guns and ammo,
> And bury me down deep below,
> Where Sid and the Buggster can't get me,
> Down where all gunnies go. Ha ha.

I feel like death, but the doctor tells me that despite my modest 40 cigarettes a day, my blood pressure of 105 over 67 is very good. It just goes to show what clean living can do.

I am sure my appeal is being delayed because Justices Zeeman, Wright and Crawford are unable to get to the Supreme Court because of the snow drifts. It is so cold that words cannot do it justice.

I was somewhat cheered up when the mail brought a letter and a lovely photo from my old mate Sherrie Sinatra, the bad girl of Australian wrestling. At 178 cm and 75 kilos, Sherrie is not the sort of girl that you would walk up to and pat on the bum.

You wouldn't be worried about the sexual harassment case, only the broken arm you were likely to get if she did not appreciate the forward move you were making. It would be a case of make a pass, and ending up on your arse.

Perhaps I could get Sherrie to come down to Launceston, tie one arm behind her back and punch up Sid Collins. Perhaps it wouldn't be fair, it might dirty Sid's frock. Fair dinkum, mentally speaking, that bloke is a rent payer, and he is about six months behind and still fighting off eviction.

Peter Warmbrunn came to see me, resplendent in his 'Glasser and Parker' suit. He is a cheeky and cheerful young scallywag and I am glad to see he is putting my fees to good use. I think sometimes there is more a touch of lout than lawyer in him.

He reminds me of a lawyer I knew in Melbourne who would spit on the ground whenever he walked past a Crown prosecutor, not that Peter would ever do such a thing – or at least get caught doing it.

I have nicknamed him Painless Pete, because as a client, when he takes your money, you don't feel a thing. Ha ha. He is a class act among the cavalcade of boring plonkers who call themselves lawyers and I predict big things for him.

1 August

I BELIEVE that the three Justices of the Tasmanian Supreme Court will return this month with the news I have been waiting for on my appeal. I will not predict which way it will go, although I am determined to take it to the High Court if we lose. I suspect that the Buggster and his team are as anxious as I am to get this settled.

There is a bit of nail biting going on in both legal camps at the moment. The truth is that neither side knows which way this will go.

For the past week I have been dreaming that I have been playing roulette and winning big. I can only hope that the dreams are good omens.

My dear old dad is in poor health and wrote to tell me that he believes that the police have been spraying his bedroom window with nerve gas. Insanity may not run in my family, but it sure as hell has been walking around near us and having a good time for a long while now.

During this trying time, it is good to have friends who want to remain loyal. A mate wrote and said that if I didn't win the appeal, I certainly wouldn't need the White Dove hanging around and he offered me a greyhound in exchange for her.

So it has come to this. Did he offer to bake me a cake with a file in it to bust out? Did he say he would write to me once a week for the rest of his life? Did he say he would hunt down the dogs who put me here? No, just wanted the address of the pretty girl who tattooed my book cover on her shoulder.

Now Karen is not mine to sell. How could he treat another human being that way? Naturally, I was outraged he could talk of exchanging a person for a dog, and I only enquired about the dog's breeding and form out of idle curiosity.

But even if I got the bloody dog, I would probably lose it to the new-fangled Confiscation of Profits of Crime Legislation which is being passed in Tasmania.

Apparently the crusaders down here have been taking my name in vain and suggesting I would be first cab off the rank. I have heard reports they intend to take the money I made out of my books and declare that it was made from crime. Well, good luck to them. If they saw my legal bills over this latest fiasco they would realise that I would have to write the Encyclopedia Britannica to even break even.

As I'm tired of explaining to these pointyheads, if I hadn't made some money out of the books then I would have got Legal Aid to pay for my two trials and the appeals and that money would have come from the public purse. At least this way, my legal battles are only a burden on me and not the public.

Furthermore, if the money I have made from writing books is considered 'profits from crime', then the writing of the books must be a crime. If that is: the case, then I demand that I be charged with the heinous offence of book writing.

Just imagine it . . . 'Mark Brandon Read, you are brought to this place to stand trial on the charge that on such and such a date, you did write a book that the membership of the Sandy Bay Yacht Club found distasteful. You are also charged with writing another book that the posh people didn't like. You are also charged with grievous bodily harm to the English language and bad literary taste.' Guilty, guilty, guilty.

Let's get on with it. Lock me up and have a little book burning to follow.

You'd have to be Linda Lovelace to swallow all that.

I will keep scribbling as long as I have something to say. The fact that my humble efforts boil the blood of so many arseholes is payment enough. Some of these clowns should remember that Oscar Wilde was a convicted criminal.

I wonder if Oscar ever had to deal with anyone like Sid Collins.

4 August

A CAVALCADE of assorted brain-dead plonkers and astronauts who call themselves lawyers in the fair city of Hobart are hanging out the windows of their various legal citadels, shaking their fists and calling for Anita Betts to be burned at the stake.

Poor little Anita would be the most unpopular lawyer in town. When lawyers get sacked and have to cop that humiliation sweet, and then watch their former clients run off and hire Anita Betts, it creates a great deal of ill-will, mutterings and mumblings down at the Old Boys' Club.

For far too long now the legal fraternity of Hobart has shuffled along doing as little as possible and getting paid far too much for doing it. They have their three-hour lunches, fill themselves with their whisky, lime and sodas, but they seem to have little concern for their poor old clients who are left in the dark about what the future holds.

I have heard lawyers down here tell prisoners that they couldn't sack them, as you can't sack a lawyer if you're on legal aid. I have heard other lawyers scream that unless the poor bugger pleaded guilty, legal aid would not grant the funding for his case. Well, if you're going to plead guilty, who needs it anyway?

The legal fraternity in Tassie is largely made up of overfed, overblown, pompous, limp-wristed, gutless, lazy, alcoholic, plead guilty, bottom-polishing arse-wipes. There are some good lawyers here, but they are in the minority. It is as if most of them don't want to rock the boat. If you are a lawyer in Tassie who works hard, puts the interest of your clients first, jumps into legal battle feet first and fights tooth and nail on behalf of the client, you are considered some sort of oddity.

The pink gin old boy brigade looks down on the hardworking lawyer who runs straight at the ball. I would reckon there would be six to eight lawyers here who could pass muster. I think the rest should be taken out and shot. In fact, I believe that the overpopulation of lawyers should be controlled by culling. Like kangaroos, if allowed to breed unchecked, they become a pest.

23 August

MONDAY night. Well, I'm off to court tomorrow. Anita and Narelle came to visit today. I thought Narelle was going to burst into tears and Anita looked nervous and anxious. Anita wanted to talk, yet she couldn't think of anything to say. She knew that the wrong word could be a jinx. Before life and death moments, you tend to become a little superstitious. I know I certainly do.

Mary-Ann arranged a special contact visit with me on Sunday. Contact visits at Risdon are not the order of the day, so it was a nice surprise. Mary-Ann is a gorgeous looking chick up close.

It made me think, many years ago I used to go out with a girl from the Reserve Bank, then there was a computer programmer from the Motor Registration Branch, then a girl from the Defence Department and Margaret from Telecom. Now there is Mary-Ann from Tax.

Maybe there is something in my personality which attracts me to public servants. Sometimes, late at night, I want to wear a cardigan and bad brown shoes. Is there flexi-time for crooks? Frightening thought, isn't it?

24 August am

IT IS Tuesday morning and all the waiting is over. The Tasmanian Supreme Court is ready and today I will be told my immediate fate. Despite my bravado I must confess that I have had an anxious night.

I wonder if it weighs heavily on the minds of judges when they know that their decisions will alter for all time the future of the people they see before them.

What I do know is that the words have already been written and their minds already made up, so there is nothing I can do about it now.

It is off to court we go to see whether the news is good or bad.

24 August pm

IT IS now over. Their Honours, Justice Zeeman, Wright and Crawford have hammered yet another nail into my legal coffin and have dismissed my appeal.

The conviction stands – for now.

I have instructed Anita to lodge another appeal against the conviction to the High Court of Australia. I remain confident that, ultimately, I will walk free.

It must be remembered amongst all the crazy legal expressions and fine Latin phrases that in the beginning I was prosecuted on the Collins matter and a jury could not make up its mind. On the second trial I was convicted on a majority verdict. The Crown could not find 12 people on a jury to agree on my guilt or innocence.

The High Court has an attitude that convictions based on majority verdicts are unsafe and unsatisfactory.

Funny thing that, so do I.

So I believe that all is not lost and this is merely a setback.

Damian Bugg, the Director of Public Prosecutions, looked as happy as a puppy with two tails when the Supreme Court came back with its decision. He was very chipper indeed.

Mary-Ann came to the jail in the afternoon because she was worried about my state of mind and heart.

My state of mind has always been questionable and my heart was broken long ago, so when you're dead inside already, it's pretty hard to inflict any further damage on yourself.

I've got a tattoo on my lower back that reads: 'I don't care if it rains or freezes, as long as I've got my plastic Jesus, sitting on the dashboard of my car.' It sums up my whole life.

When the appeal was thrown out, the members of the press present looked pleased. As I stood in the dock like a chocolate teapot as their Honours hit my appeal for six, the media representatives looked as if they were about to break out in song.

It is funny, but I learned long ago that the media love to hate me in public, yet they want to stick their tongues in my mouth in private.

It is all part of the tragic comedy which goes to make up my life.

Two of Dynamic Damian's legal helpers, who I have named 'Bill and Ben, the flowerpot men', danced a jig of delight outside the court. From all reports, I hope they are better lawyers than dancers.

There was much back slapping and three cheers for the Buggster. Good luck to him, he won the day, but this is a 15-rounder and a glancing blow early in the fight will be of no consequence when the final bell sounds.

Anita marched down the court steps to tell the waiting media her client was innocent and an appeal would go to the High Court, bless her black stockings.

Everyone seems to be having a jolly good time at my expense, but you don't toss the party until the body has been burned, and I ain't dead yet.

One of the best legal brains about is a chap named David Porter, and he is the man we want to handle the next legal battle. I have had a sneaky eye on him for some time.

In the High Court you need brains, cool nerves, quick wits and a thought process like a legal library. Porter lectures in law. The High Court is no place for fan dancers and fire eaters.

Anyway, the opera ain't over till someone shoots the fat lady. Until then, Je Ne Regrette Rien.

27 August

I BELIEVE that Mr David Porter will handle my appeal. He is a top lawyer with a great legal mind and I have every faith that we will eventually dispense with this legal rubbish.

I am in legal custody as a result of an officially sanctioned rigged-up jury system. The majority verdict rule was put into place by some of the state's law makers. I imagine the thinking at the time was to stop the guilty from escaping justice. But I think the rule also means that the innocent don't have much chance either.

I think you could call it a sort of courtroom gerrymander, stacking the deck, jury wise. It may be legal, but it is hardly fair play. I am no legal expert, at best I am a jailhouse lawyer, but even I am aware that the High Court of Australia is not keen on majority verdicts.

The High Court said the principle that the verdict of a jury in a criminal trial should be by the agreement of all jurors dated back to the 14th century and was assumed to be the case when the Constitution was drawn up at the beginning of the century.

Down here in the deep south, it doesn't seem to matter.

Let's put it this way: If 12 doctors examined your mother and 10 said she was dead and two said she was very much alive would you accept the majority opinion and ring the undertaker, or sack the lot and get a new medical team? You cannot sign a death certificate under Australian law unless the patient is 100 per cent dead. If any doctor came to you and said, 'Sorry, but we buried your dear old granny yesterday. The old girl was about 90 per cent dead any, rate, so bugger it, what's the difference?', you would not be impressed.

Thank goodness that majority verdicts aren't used in the public hospital system. If the Tasmanian majority verdict method was used in hospitals, anything worse than a broken leg and we would all be dead as door nails in no time flat.

August 31

IT APPEARS that David Porter has only agreed to advise on the case so it may be that the Mouth from the South, Michael Hodgeman, may be the man to fly the flag for me in the final hearing. He is a top bloke and although he appears to be a mate of the Buggster, I will not hold that against either of them. After all, it is Tasmania.

Anita tells me that Mr Hodgeman has a brilliant legal mind and backs it up with a heap of dash. He seems to be the man for me in this sort of mess.

I remain convinced that I can win this. I noticed that, in dismissing my appeal, Justice Zeeman said that the trial judge had erred in his direction to the jury, yet Justice Zeeman said, 'I am satisfied that no substantial miscarriage of justice has actually occurred by reason of the misdirection.'

I am left to wonder what level of a miscarriage of justice is considered acceptable. Apparently it has to be a 'substantial' miscarriage before it matters.

I hope the High Court will have other ideas.

I know there are people who would be as delighted as a pack of poofters in a Vaseline factory if I shut up and stayed in jail. But I will not be silenced. I remain the greatest living writer with no ears in the world.

Such is life.

The last word?

So now you've read my third book,
It really should be the last,
For a bloke who can't spell too good,
I write the buggers fast.
But maybe in time to come,
When I've got more to tell,
I might just take pen in hand,
And give the numbnuts hell.
But for now, I'll wave goodbye,
And quietly fade away,
Writing gives me a headache,
And I'm calling it a day.
But if the legal bills keep mounting,
And you really do want more,
Bugger it, what the hell?
I might write Chopper Four.
Ha ha